The Integrated Elementary Classroom

A Developmental Model of Education for the 21st Century

Manon P. Charbonneau

Associate Professor of Education and Director of Student Teaching
College of Santa Fe

Barbara E. Reider

Assistant Professor of Education and Education Department Chair
College of Santa Fe

Allyn and Bacon
Boston • London • Toronto • Sydney • Tokyo • Singapore

Series Editor: Virginia Lanigan
Production Administrator: Joe Sweeney
Editorial-Production Service: Barbara J. Barg
Cover Administrator: Suzanne Harbison
Manufacturing Buyer: Louise Richardson
Composition Buyer: Linda Cox

Library of Congress Cataloging-in-Publication Data

Chabonneau, Manon P.
    The integrated elementary classroom: a developmental model of
education for the twenty-first century/Manon P. Charbonneau,
Barbara E. Reider.
        p. cm.
    Includes bibliographical references and index.
    ISBN 0-205-15462-X (pbk.)
    1. Nongraded schools—United States.   2. Teacher-student
relationships—United States.   3. Education, Elementary—United
States.   4. Child Development—United States.   5. Cognitive styles
in children—United States.   I. Reider, Barbara.   II. Title.
LB1029.N6C46   1995
371.2'54—dc20   94-33078
                                                            CIP

Printed in the United States of America
10 9 8 7 6 5 4 3 2 1   99 98 97 96 95 94

*To our students at the College of Santa Fe,
our colleagues in the Education Department,
teachers in the Santa Fe Public Schools,
and our families.*

photo by Ben Montague

Manon P. Charbonneau is currently an Associate Professor of Elementary Education and the Director of Student Teaching in the Department of Education at the College of Santa Fe. Dr. Charbonneau recieved her Ph.D. from the University of New Mexico in Curriculum and Instruction in Multicultural Teacher Education. In 1992, she was the CASE Professor of the Year for the State of New Mexico. She also has directed a teacher center in Santa Fe, and worked as a curriculum consultant on the Hopi Reservation in Hortevilla, Arizona.

Barbara E. Reider recieved her Ph.D. from Bryn Mawr in Human Development and also holds degrees in elementary education and educational psychology. After teaching in an urban area of Philadelphia, she consulted to a variety of educational programs and taught as adjunct faculty at Temple University, Beaver College, and Trenton State College before coming to the College of Santa Fe where she currently is the Chairperson for the Education Department. Dr. Reider is a National Certified School Psychologist and and belongs to the National Association of School Psychologist, the American Education Research Association, the Association for Supervision and Curriculum Development, and the Phi Delta Kappa.

Contents

Introduction: Setting the Stage

What We Are About

This book is about schools and about children IN schools. This book is also about teachers: their knowledge, attitudes and decision-making as they affect the classroom environment and interactions between child and teacher. This book focuses on developing children who are competent, responsible learners who have the skills and abilities to succeed in the twenty-first century. It is a book about building resiliency in children by capitalizing on their strengths.

Students everywhere are "firing" schools at an extraordinarily high rate: literally, by physically dropping out, and psychologically, by detaching themselves from the classroom process. Although we tend to focus on the physical dropout problems, it is the students who psychologically dropout as early as kindergarten who require our immediate and constant attention. By the time a student who has had a history of school failure and non-responsive classroom experiences reaches the eighth grade, interventions are often less effective.

Because of the importance of early intervention, we have chosen to focus on the elementary school-age child, 5 to 12 years old. We believe that through responsive, developmentally appropriate classroom experiences using a holistic, coherent curriculum, children will stay engaged in learning and make significant cognitive and social/emotional gains. The purpose of this book is to provide a framework and specific guidelines for creating such a classroom environment.

How This Approach Relates to Today's Children: the At-risk Society

It has been said that the structure of the American school, as it exists today, serves only about twenty percent of the population successfully, although the many definitions of *successfully* automatically preclude accurate statistics. The current surge of restructuring movements across the country is a clear indication of considerable concern from all sectors of our society that schools are in trouble.

Not only are there problems inherent in an outdated school system, but there are also problems that an inordinate number of today's children bring to school. These put them further at risk for not receiving the necessary educational experience. Many of today's children come from situations that include dysfunctional families, alcoholism and drug abuse, physical and emotional abuse, poverty, homelessness, and alienation from the mainstream of society. Most of these problems occur at all socioeconomic levels. Brendtro, Brokenleg and Van Bockern (1990) describe the phenomenon of being at risk as arising from destructive relationships, climates of futility, learned irresponsibility and a loss of purpose. Keith Geiger, president of the National Education Association, states the following:

> *America's children are in trouble. One of every four children under the age of six is growing up in poverty. Twelve million children have no medical insurance. America's infant mortality rate is higher than Singapore's. Children are abused, neglected and denied access to quality early childhood programs. Kindergarten teachers report that a third of the children in their classrooms arrive at school ill-prepared to learn.*
>
> *A year ago, the National Commission on Children . . . called it "a tragic irony that the most prosperous nation on earth is failing so many of its children." Nothing has changed over the past year. The irony remains. The tragedy grows. America continues to fail millions of its children. . . .*
>
> *The problems of children today pose a real threat to America's tomorrow. If our government cannot take he lead in solving those problems—cannot safeguard our nation's children and our future—what is its purpose? . . . Children's future and America's future are being formed today. Neither can wait. (Geiger, Making Children a Priority: a message from the National Education Association 1992)*

Schools, through non-responsive environments, low expectations, and an inability and unwillingness to treat each child as an individual with specific learning needs add to the problems that the child may already have, increasing the probability of putting that child at risk for school failure. Competitive classrooms which alienate children from each other and promote feelings of inadequacy are examples of at-risk climates. In homogeneous, traditional classrooms (same age groups or tracked sections), students have little opportunity for helping peers, developing leadership qualities, or developing a sense of responsibility for their own learning as well as that of others. In classrooms where curriculum is irrelevant and fragmented—for example, when strict adherence to texts and workbooks is emphasized, when skills are learned in isolation, and when rigid time frames are adhered to—there is usually little sense that what is being learned is useful outside of those four walls. According to Brendtro et al., "today, we have a greater stake in achieving success for all children. The costs of supporting drop outs and dump outs as illiterate, unemployable, violent or mentally ill citizens are staggering. We can no longer afford the economic drain of disposable people." (Brendtro et al., 1990, p. 3)

Reducing The Risk Factors: Creating Resiliency

Schools have many opportunities to create climates that will foster resiliency and reduce the factors that put children at risk. The term *resilient* refers to the capacity to spring back from and/or successfully adapt to adversity (Success Through Partnerships, Albuquerque Public Schools 1992). The Western Regional Center (1991) points to several factors which enable children to succeed despite monumental odds. Their definition of the resilient child is one who has social competence, problem-solving skills, and an internal locus of control. These characteristics significantly reverse or decrease the impact of risk factors and involve the caring and support of peers, friends and teachers, high expectations, and participation and involvement in all aspects of school and community. In *Reclaiming Youth at Risk* (Brendtro et al., 1990), the authors describe environments that reduce risk factors as those with ample opportunities to belong, to develop a sense of independence, to give to others, and to gain a sense of mastery.

The Integrated Approach

The approach presented in this book is designed to build resiliency and reduce risk factors by creating classrooms that foster a strong sense of community and provide many opportunities for critical thinking and choice, experiences in working cooperatively with others, and time to develop personal strengths, self knowledge and competencies in all areas of development. These classrooms can provide many of the necessary components for mending or greatly reducing the impact of societal and institutional at-risk conditions. Resiliency factors are encouraged through the use of an approach that helps to ensure each child's success.

The integrated approach requires that teachers utilize (1) developmental principles as the underlying basis for all teacher decision making, (2) multi-age groupings to underscore "real world" learning and working conditions, (3) cooperative learning models to encourage interdependency and socially appropriate, altruistic behavior, (4) a relevant, coherent curriculum, and (5) a direct application of the theory of multiple intelligences (Gardner, 1983, 1991, 1993), which speak to individual differences and to children's ways of learning.

An integrated approach supports individual learning styles and developmental growth patterns: physical, cognitive, psychological and social. It is a philosophy of teaching and learning that assumes that ALL children can and will learn what society expects, within a framework of careful guidance and direct teaching when necessary and appropriate. There is no failure in an integrated approach, only different degrees of success based on different developmental levels. The integrated approach changes the role of the teacher from dispenser of knowledge to catalyst, coach, and guide.

An integrated approach also includes many of the restructuring principles that are guiding the redesigning of today's schools (Sizer's RE: LEARNING, Johnson and Johnson's Cooperative Learning, Levin's Accelerated Schools, Comer's model for urban schools, Lezotte's Effective Schools model, and others). All these models place the child at the center of the learning process. All require teachers to understand their classrooms in vastly different ways. Almost all are based on principles of critical and creative thinking, responsiveness to differences in learning styles, active participation on the part of the student in the learning process, relevancy of curriculum, and an understanding of concepts as interconnected in a world where knowledge can no longer be fragmented and compartmentalized.

There are many debates as to what should be the outcome of schooling in our society today. The "successful" school is defined differently by different groups and individuals. Often "success" is related to academic achievement as determined by standardized tests or by how many children from a particular school are accepted and attend prestigious colleges. For some, a successful school is one which prepares students for the competitive world of work, and provides them with skills required in the workplace. For some parents, success may mean that their child is a straight "A" student, while for others, it is the development of intellectual skills as well as social competency. For some teachers, "success" is engaging all children, while for others, it is meeting the needs of the very bright. Children often see schools from an entirely different perspective. A "successful" school for some students is a place to be with friends, to be off the streets, and to get by without being noticed. For others, a "successful" school gives them the opportunity for leadership either scholastically, socially, and athletically; sometimes for all three.

This book takes the position that a successful school experience is one that fosters a life-long love of learning, and a perceived sense of self as competent and able to direct and control one's life. Our working definition of "success," therefore, is as follows:

1. children who have developed a sense of their own competency as a social, cognitive beings.
2. children who understand the relevancy of what they are learning in the classroom to life in the "real world."
3. children who can apply what they learn in the classroom to that "real world."
4. children who can make decisions comfortably and trust in their own ability to do so.
5. children who have an ability to question thoughtfully and creatively.
6. children who have developed adequate problem-solving skills.
7. children who have realistic but high expectations for their own performance.

How This Book Is Organized

The first six chapters begin with two scenarios that contrast a traditional classroom with one that is using an integrated approach. We have consciously made these scenarios extreme in order to point out the major differences in approaches. In reality, many classrooms fall on a continuum between these two extremes. Much of our material has been gathered from teachers, and our examples come directly from classrooms in process. We focus a great deal of attention on teacher decision making, in order to help the reader to better understand the less obvious variables that determine classroom outcomes, from how the physical environment is created to ways of assessing student progress through performance and portfolio.

Each chapter of this book is designed to look at a specific aspect of the integrated approach and teacher decision making as it relates to that aspect. The last two chapters bring together all of these aspects so that the reader will have a more comprehensive understanding of how the pieces fit together. Throughout the book concrete examples are provided which demonstrate how the integrated approach can be implemented.

We suggest that each reader who already uses an integrated approach, or intends to use it, keep a three-ring notebook with dividers titled to match our chapters. Into this notebook then can go any current articles from professional journals or any other references which might help and guide the teacher as he or she begins or expands implementation of an integrated classroom.

Acknowledgements

We would like to acknowledge all the teachers in the field, and our students at The College of Santa Fe who contributed to this manuscript as well as the reviewers who provided helpful feedback and suggestions to this manuscript: Linda Grippando; Stan Chu, Bank Street College of Education; Sue Whitten, Ralph Wheelock School; Dawna Lisa Buchanan-Berrigan, Shawnee State University; Thomas Lasley, University of Dayton; Joan Duea, University of Northern Iowa; and Delores Gardner, Texas Women's University. We wish to especially acknowledge our editor at Allyn and Bacon, Virginia Lanigan, and our technical editor, Barbara J. Barg.

References

Brendtro, Larry K., Brokenleg, Martin, and Van Bockern, Steve. (1990). *Reclaiming Youth at Risk*. Bloomington: National Education Service.

Gardner, Howard. (1983). *Frames of Mind*. New York: Basic Books.

Gardner, Howard. (1991). *The Unschooled Mind*. New York: Basic Books.

Gardner, Howard (1993). *Multiple Intelligences: The Theory in Practice*. New York: Basic Books.

Geiger, Keith. (1992). "Making Children a Priority." Editorial, National Education Association, Washington D.C.

Western Regional Center: Drug Free Schools and Communities. (1991). *Fostering Resiliency; Protective Factors in the Family, School and Community*.

Bibliography

Brookover, W.B., Beamer, L., Efthim,H., Hathaway, D., Lezotte, L., Miller, S., Passalacqua, J., and Tornatzky, L. (1982). *Creating Effective Schools: An In-service Program for Enhancing School Learning, Climate and Achievements*. Florida: Learning Publications.

Comer, James. (1990). *School Power: Implications of an Interactive Project*. New York: The Free Press.

Johnson, David W. and Johnson, Roger T. (1984). *Circles of Learning*. Virginia: Association for Supervision and Curriculum Development.

Johnson, David W. and Johnson, Roger T. (1991). *Learning Together and Alone*. Boston: Allyn and Bacon.

Johnson, David W. and Johnson, Frank P. (1991). *Joining Together*. Englewood Cliffs: Prentice-Hall.

Resources

Comer, James P. Yale Child Study Center, P.O. Box 3333, New Haven, Connecticut 06510.

Gardner, Howard. Harvard Project Zero, Harvard Graduate School of Education, 323 Longfellow Hall, Appian Way, Cambridge, Massachusetts 02138.

Levin, Henry. The Accelerated Schools Project, Stanford University, CERAS Building, Stanford, California 94305-3084.

Lezotte, Lawrence. Effective Schools, 2199 Jolly Road, Suite 169, Okemos, Michigan 48864.

Sizer, Theodore. The Coalition of Essential Schools, Box 1969, Brown University, Providence, Rhode Island 02912.

A Historical and Theoretical Perspective

Being bottled up for seven hours a day, in a place where you decide nothing, having your success or failure depend, a hundred times a day, on the plan, invention, and whim of someone else, being put in a position where most of your real desires are not only ignored but actively penalized, undertaking nothing for its own sake but only for that illusory carrot of the future—maybe you can do it, and maybe you can't, but either way, it's probably done you some harm. (Herndon, 1971, p. 96)

Most of us have in mind a vision of having spent about 10,000 hours in an elementary/secondary school environment characterized in the above quotation. For some of us, this environment truly prepared us for our adult lives. For others, it was a crushing blow to our spirits and continued interest as learners. Regardless of the effect on the individual, there was a time in our society when such an environment was considered necessary to ready the individual for the "factory model" of work.

Today, we have a much different society, one which requires an individual to have complex reasoning skills, self-direction and self-knowledge, creativity, and the ability to work cooperatively with others for solutions to the problems facing the twenty-first century. Schools, therefore, must change to address the needs of today's society and tomorrow's global community. To accomplish this vision, schools need to recognize the value of the individual child in new ways that take into consideration each child's particular ways of learning and knowing, interests, and inner ability to create knowledge and make decisions with the assistance of teacher and peers.

The window into two classrooms pictures two radically different philosophies of learning. These philosophies take a very different perspective of the child as learner, and of the teacher's role in the classroom. Classroom 1 is characteristic of the classroom of yesterday. Classroom 2 is the model that has the potential for achieving the needs of children moving into the twenty-first century.

A Window into Two Classrooms

Classroom 1: A Traditional Environment of First-Graders

Children in this classroom are sitting at individual desks, facing the teacher who stands in front of the class. The teacher keeps reminding children to pay attention—"I need your eyes up here," "I'm waiting for Elizabeth," "Watch carefully as I write the words"—as she presents a list of spelling words. Quite a few of the children are busy looking under and into their desks, playing with their shoelaces or items from their supplies. Only about half of the twenty-five children are "ready" to copy the spelling words as the teacher lists them on the chalkboard. The teacher is becoming more and more agitated as this lesson must be completed before beginning required reading groups on time. She had hoped to give the children time to copy each word five times, providing them needed practice in spelling before moving on to reading; however, time is slipping away.

The teacher is wondering why the children cannot sit up straight, pay attention, and stay focused on such a necessary component of the curriculum. Don't *all* children have to learn to spell specific words if they are to read and write at grade level by the end of the year? Isn't it easier and more efficient to teach a needed skill or concept to the whole class at the same time? Aren't all six-year-olds cognitively developed at approximately the same level? Why did the kindergarten teacher pass along children who were not "ready" for first grade? I used the same plans last year, which worked pretty well for my first year of teaching. I'm doing the same thing I did before: why isn't it working this time? There must be something the matter with this group of children.

Classroom 2: An Integrated Multi-Age Environment of Children 5, 6, and 7 Years Old

Children are scattered all over the room, some at tables but many on the floor on pillows and mats. Upon entering the room, the teacher is virtually hidden. With closer inspection, she can be found on the floor with a small group of children, some 5 years old, some 6, and some 7, going over their personalized spelling notebooks.

Each child's words have been taken from their journals and creative writing. Initially, children utilized invented spelling in their writing. (*Invented spelling* is a method of encouraging the child to spell words exactly as they sound to him or her.) For example, Peter has spelled his own name PDR, which is a typical first attempt at spelling since children hear only consonants at first. As children have more experience with the written and spoken word, they begin to hear, and write, the more subtle vowel sounds. The teacher in this classroom recognizes the developmental stages of the writing process, and understands that invented spelling allows children to write freely and creatively without pressure to spell accurately as they get down their important thoughts. The teacher also knows that young children cannot focus on two concepts simultaneously: getting their thoughts written down *and* using correct spelling. The teacher believes that, for these children, the most immediate goal is for them to trust that their ideas are important and valuable, and that putting them on paper is the first step to communicating these ideas to others. Children in this class know that to communicate through writing with others, they eventually will need to use traditional orthography (standard spellings), but they also know that the first step is writing something interesting that others will want to read. These children know that editing their work is a critical step in becoming good writers, and they look forward to their session with the teacher. Learning the standard spellings becomes a shared experience in the group as they notice words in common to be practiced.

Children who are not working directly with the teacher are busy writing, reading alone or in pairs, working on math problems of interest, or observing and noting how their plants are growing. There is the low, quiet hum throughout the room of children talking quietly with each other. The teacher in this classroom knows that children develop their skills at different rates and have different interests that can foster those skills. She expects that children will seek opportunities to write and to read about what they are doing even if their levels of achievement are vastly different. The teacher had a very different group of children in her last year's class. Although two-thirds of the children are the same this year, at the beginning of the year the new children to the class were, on the whole, more mature and more able to direct their own activity. The teacher, through careful observation and assessment, recognized that the children new to the group were ready for certain experiences earlier in the term. The teacher was able to utilize the broad concepts from last year's goals and objectives, but the implementation had to be adjusted to fit the needs of her current group.

The Integrated Approach

Background

The integrated approach, as described in this book, has been influenced by several historical benchmarks in educational change. The thread that ties these changes together is a child-centered classroom where the individual needs and interests of children are of primary focus. This implies a carefully developed curriculum, classroom environment, and teacher-student interactions, the goal of which is to create self-motivated, responsible learners.

Early Influences

As early as the middle of the eighteenth century there were educational philosophers, such as Rousseau and Pestalozzi, and somewhat later, John Dewey, who espoused the importance of a curriculum emphasizing the needs and interest of the learner. Dewey, in *Experience and Education* (1938, p. 88) states that "it is a cardinal principle of education that the beginning of instruction shall be made with the experience learners already have; that this experience and the capacities that have been developed during its course provide the starting point for all further learning." The school curriculum devised at Dewey's Laboratory School at the University of Chicago became the resource for many progressive educators and the prototype for the experimental progressive school. Dewey's philosophy was a major force in the progressive education movement.

According to Saylor, Alexander, and Lewis, the Association for the Advancement of Progressive Education, which was formed in 1919, believed that the fullest development of the individual was based on a scientific study of the individual's mental, physical, spiritual, and social characteristics and needs. The views of this association, which was later called the Progressive Education Association, were governed by the following principles:

1. Freedom to develop naturally.
2. Interest the motive of all work.
3. The teacher a guide, not a taskmaster.
4. Scientific study of pupil development.
5. Greater attention to all that affects the child's physical development.
6. Cooperation between school and home to meet the needs of child-life.
7. The progressive school a leader in educational movement. (Saylor et al., 1981, p. 241)

After World War II, the British primary educational system, more so than the educational system in the United States, followed through on the philosophy inherent in the Progressive Education movement. This strong emphasis on the child as the center of the learning process was a major component of the educational philosophy of the British long before World War II. However, during World War II, literally thousands of British children were evacuated from the large cities, which were the relentless targets of German bombing raids, to the country for safety. It was here that children lived in groups with teachers in what would be considered a boarding school situation. While some teachers were able to continue their professional role in these boarding schools, many more found themselves in factories or in the armed services. Changes in the demographic makeup of the country, the loss of large numbers of teachers to the war effort, and changes in family life required a restructuring of the educational system. Remaining teachers were not only responsible for creating new learning environments, but also for creating a sense of "family" and security within a new living arrangement. Teachers in this situation found themselves to be the true "alma mater" to their young charges.

Schools at this time were makeshift, usually without the textbooks they had been using and largely without materials of any kind. The villages and towns became the classroom and curriculum. Children studied the physical environment: the bridges, buildings, parks, brooks, ponds and rivers, hedgerows, and even the cemeteries. Teachers had children working cooperatively in groups: if a particular historic building was the focus, some researched the history of the gate, while others focused on the building itself. Still others spent their time understanding the tree and plant growth surrounding the building. Children were challenged to find out as much as possible about their particular area of research after which the findings were shared.

Due to the successes of these new, more informal, approaches to education, changes in teacher beliefs about teaching and learning occurred, so that after the war, many of these "new" methodologies were incorporated into the British curriculum. From these simple beginnings evolved *thematic* or *interdisciplinary* instruction. Teachers and children would select a topic of interest to pursue throughout a term, and this topic would include concepts and skills from the traditional curriculum. This approach was found to be a humane, efficient, and exciting instructional strategy in which children learned to apply to a real problem the skills formerly learned in isolation. Children also learned to apply ideas, skills, and concepts learned in one context to other areas of study. Clearly, the focus was child-centered, with the belief that if a child is interested in some topic, he or she will learn. Thematic instruction afforded teachers a natural, logical way to incorporate instructional strategies that were later demonstrated by research to be effective. These included cooperative learning, child as researcher, and teacher as facilitator or "coach" (Humphreys, Post, and Ellis, 1992).

After the war, it became necessary to depart from a strictly formal presentation of subject matter because of the large numbers of children assigned to one teacher. Class size in state schools was dictated to be forty children to one teacher. Teachers realized that delivery of curriculum content in the traditional way was not going to work for most children. With such large numbers in each classroom, there had to be a way in which children could be involved as active learners. In place of having a classroom of one specific age level, teachers felt that multi-age, "family," or vertical groupings of children could impact their instructional strategies positively. For example, older children could work with younger ones while the teacher met with a small group needing specific guidance, direct teaching, or skills practice. Family groupings were particularly important in the British primary schools because they provided a transition for children from home to school. Children stayed in the same group from age five through age seven, sharing a common community of tradition and culture.

> *In the vertical grouped class, the child is working with others his own age, with younger and older children, with children of differing abilities, interests, social and economic backgrounds. He is one member of a mixed society, which, by the time he joins it has become a very natural "family" group. . . . The children do not spend much of their time testing the bounds of what is allowed and what is not—finding out how far they can go— because they are soon made aware of the limits not just by the teacher but by the established members of the class. (Brown and Precious, 1968, p. 44)*

Vertical groupings encouraged children to work in interest groups rather than just friendship groups, providing more opportunity for an individual child to develop his or her optimum potential. Teachers could provision the environment according to children's changing needs: adding materials, adding to the complexity of existing materials, and providing new activities and projects. Vertical grouping was then extended to the eight-, nine- and ten-year-old "intermediate" levels because of the successes in the primary classrooms.

Interest in an approach to education which more carefully considered how children changed and developed over time was stronger in postwar England than it was in the United States. Particularly influenced by Jean Piaget, the integrated day classroom emerged. "The Integrated Day could be described as a school day which is combined into a whole and has the minimum of timetabling. Within this day there is time and opportunity in a planned educative environment for the social, emotional, physical and aesthetic growth of the child at his own rate of development." (Brown and Precious, 1968, pp. 12, 13) This type of classroom focussed on the changing cognitive needs of individual children and helped guide teachers in the use of alternative strategies in their approach to teaching. It was better understood in England that for children to fully develop as individuals, the total classroom environment had to provide for exploration and interaction with others. Children's interests and skills, as well as their way of understanding their "world," changed as the child grew and developed. "In the integrated day classroom, the child is choosing his own task, developing at his own rate and working to his own best standard." (Brown and Precious, 1968, p. 39) The United States at that time was still tied very closely to the behaviorist school of psychology. This approach emphasized the curriculum over the child with little concern for individual differences. It took the position that the child is an empty receptacle and that the teacher's job was to fill up the receptacle with a prescribed body of knowledge.

Another factor which influenced changes in many schools throughout England was the autonomous nature of the Local Education Authority (LEA), an established practice in British state schools since World War I. School heads, also called head teachers, had the authority to choose not only what was to be taught, but how. Wise head teachers always consulted other teachers in the school as did the LEAs, which made them all hold a stake in the process of change. This process of inclusion is a major component of many of the restructuring movements occurring today. In those schools in which the integrated day was being established, rarely were decisions made behind closed doors by administrators (Blackie, 1967, 1971). At that time, the integrated day was limited to smaller schools in more rural areas.

Later Influences

> At the heart of the educational process lies the child. No advances in poli-
> cy, no acquisitions of new equipment have their desired effect, unless they
> are in harmony with the nature of the child, unless they are fundamental-
> ly acceptable to him. We know a little about what happens to the child who
> is deprived of the stimuli of pictures, books and spoken words: we know
> much less about what happens to a child who is exposed to stimuli which
> are perceptually, intellectually, or emotionally inappropriate to his age, his
> state of development, or the sort of individual he is. (The Plowden Report
> of the Central Advisory Council for Education, England: Her Majesty's
> Stationery Office, 1967, p. 7)

The quotation that begins this paragraph was written in 1967 in a historic document which played a critical role in the continued educational reform of many British primary schools, and strengthened the use of methodologies in place in those classrooms already using the integrated day. The Plowden Report is as crucial and applicable today as it was at the time it was written. This document was titled *Children and Their Primary Schools* and was commissioned by the Ministry of Education for the Central Advisory Council for Education. Lady Bridget Plowden chaired the commission.

The Plowden Report made recommendations in many areas of primary education, focusing specifically on: (1) children's growth and development, (2) the importance of the learning environment, (3) participation by parents in the child's education, and (4) the particular needs of children whose culture differed from that of children in the mainstream culture. The recommendations from this report defined the child as a unique individual with great strength and enormous capacities for learning, as well as a wealth of intuitive ideas already in hand for how the world works. The Plowden Report wielded enormous influence over how children were taught in England, and has also influenced the educational experience of children in the United States, beginning in the early seventies when the Plowden Report became more common reading among educators in this country.

The Plowden Report supported a child-centered classroom, basing many of its findings on good child development theory, careful and insightful observation of classrooms, and input from teachers throughout the country. Without a doubt, it became a "bible" for model primary education in Great Britain. The Plowden Report provided a survey of the status of early education in England, proposals for needed educational reform, and also favorable references to classroom procedures followed in about one-third of the primary schools. These procedures were seen as resulting from a tradition of "revolution." The key elements of this tradition included: (1) a latitude of freedom among school personnel to determine the contents of a curriculum, (2) a gradual shifting of the role of government officials responsible for overseeing public education from evaluators to advisors, and (3) the reliance on contemporary developmental psychology as a way of understanding children's learning and motivation. Piagetian psychology is most widely accepted as the source of these insights (Evans, 1975).

The schools identified in the Plowden Report as providing the most effective education were those that shared certain commonalities: the integrated day, vertical (family or multi-age) grouping, and a greater emphasis on inductive thinking and the development of problem-solving strategies. In addition, there was particular avoidance of the work/play dichotomy so firmly entrenched in traditional schools.

The integrated day was possibly the most significant outcome of the British education movement. Because of the nature of the integrated day, lessons typically did not fit into a prescribed time allotment. Classrooms were organized into learning areas for particular activities such as reading and writing, science and math, and the visual arts. Children were encouraged to accept responsibility for their own learning experiences. They were permitted to follow their interests and take as long as they needed to explore a particular activity. The teacher's main role was to plan skillfully, and to organize the learning areas with the children's assistance. The physical arrangements of the classrooms were less important than the freedom to experiment with these arrangements.

When a class of seven-year-olds notice(s) the birds that come to the bird table outside the classroom window, they may decide, after discussion with their teacher, to make their own aviary. They will set to, with a will, and paint the birds in flight, make models of them in clay or papier-mache, write stories and poems about them and look up reference books to find out more about their habits. Children are not assimilating inert ideas, but are wholly involved in thinking, feeling and doing. The slow and bright share a common experience and each takes from it what he can at his own level. There is no attempt to put reading and writing into separate compartments: both serve a wider purpose and artificial barriers do not fragment the learning experience. (Plowden, 1967, p. 199)

Not all of the schools surveyed in the Plowden Report utilized vertical or family grouping. However, it was found that those schools making use of such groupings made it possible for cross sections of an entire school population to be represented in each classroom. Teachers of these classes reported that this organization emphasized individuality rather than hiding it under the cloak of artificial age groupings, ability groupings, or both (Evans, 1975).

The focus on inductive thinking and problem-solving skills encouraged a process-oriented rather than a product-oriented curriculum. How children approached their learning environment, how they made use of available materials, and how they synthesized their own learning became one of the focuses of education. Play was seen as the principal means of learning for young children. Little emphasis was placed on what a child was going to do with learning in the future; more important was making the best use of the child's present learning situation.

Another component of the British model was team teaching. The teachers worked together, utilizing each others' strengths. In addition, schools emphasized the importance of harmonious school–parent relationships. Parents were apprised of school practices and visitation in classrooms was encouraged.

The idea of child-centered classrooms flew across the waters and took the United States by storm in the sixties; however the strengths of the Plowden Report (its careful study of good developmental theory and its implications for practice in the classroom) did not. Child-centered classrooms became a fad with little regard for the underlying philosophy and theory. The open education movement in the United States was born and became synonymous with permissiveness and lack of academic rigor.

Terms such as *open classrooms, free schools,* and *integrated classrooms* were used interchangeably as examples of the open education movement. The unrest of the sixties supported the open education frenzy. A string of books criticizing American education began with John Holt's book *How Children Fail* (Holt, 1964). Other books, such as *36 Children* (Kohl, 1967), *Death at an Early Age* (Kozol, 1967), *The Lives of Children* (Dennison, 1969), and *The Way It Spozed To Be* (Herndon, 1965) all supported the notion that our educational system was in crisis and change was necessary. The new child-centered approaches associated with open education were seen as a panacea. Architects began designing schools with few interior walls and partitions to support the notion of an "open" classroom in which children could freely interact with each other and with materials. Teachers were asked to utilize this new concept of space without the recognition that an open classroom is a philosophy of learning and teaching, not a result of architectural construction. Teachers in many cases were told to change their teaching techniques to "open classroom style." For many, training and guidance in these new theories of learning were simply a series of unrelated strategies that had no real underlying substance. Teachers were not given direction as to how to plan curriculum to meet the needs of children in an open classroom environment. The environment dictated curriculum and teacher behavior. Post-secondary teacher education programs were slow to alter their method of preparing teachers to be successful in a non-traditional classroom.

The open education movement failed in this country, dismally and relatively quickly. Parents were not adequately prepared for the physical or curricular changes that were taking place. Teachers found that just putting children in large open learning areas with a large quantity of equipment did not produce the discovery of concepts, the mastery of skills, or the independent learner that had been the watchwords of open education. School leaders who encouraged careful and critical study of the British primary school brought British teachers to this country for extensive workshops on the integrated day philosophy. Teachers who were able to take part in these workshops were more likely to make appropriate changes in their classrooms. The child-centered movement survived mainly in small, independent schools across the United States. It was easier for change to occur in the smaller entities than in the large school systems and within the private rather than the public sector.

Criticisms of the Child-Centered Movement

In January 1992, the *London Times* (*The Sunday Times*, January 26, 1992 Focus 1.9) published a lengthy article decrying the enormous influence of the Plowden Report on British education over the previous twenty-five years. "The Great Betrayal" claims that the Plowden Report was responsible for blighting the country's schools for a generation. However, a careful reading of the article reveals that the criticism is unsupported. Similarly, a recent government inquiry into the need for the reinstitution of more traditional classroom methods does not support this criticism. Maurice Kogan, Inquiry Secretary, is quoted in this *London Times* article as saying "The (Plowden) Report tilted distinctly toward discovery. . . and away from the structured and that which might be transmitted through firm and perhaps standardized learning routines. This could be done badly and be a cop-out by teachers . . . perhaps the best ideals of education are just too difficult for all or most." Jacobs (1989, pp. 17, 18) states that the integrated day model, as practiced in British primary schools and some schools in the United States, "represents a philosophy that is not held by many teachers, and they must believe it for it to work effectively." She goes on to say that "the approach entails enormous work and planning by teachers because it is not based on an existing curriculum. The management of classroom organization is highly sophisticated and requires specific training." Without a doubt this is a correct assessment, but it does not and should not preclude interested teachers from becoming effective educators in such an integrated environment.

A misunderstanding of the open education movement and the integrated approach has led to a belief that open education implies permissiveness—license, if you will, to do as one pleases all day long. However, nowhere in any of the literature that supports child-centered classrooms is the suggestion made that children do not need to learn to read, write, and do mathematics. The thoughtful, well-planned, child-centered classroom takes the position that there are better ways for children to learn than those found in more traditional classrooms. The two classrooms described at the beginning of this chapter emphasize the differences in approaches and underlying beliefs in how children learn. There have been, and continue to be, two major schools of thought as to how children learn. One is based on the idea that children only learn with direct instruction, with curriculum carefully sequenced in a specific way. The other posits that children construct their own knowledge by interacting with each other, knowledgeable adults, and with appropriate materials. This second school of thought also supports the idea that children learn in vastly different ways.

Advocates of the first school of thought talk about the need to go "back to basics." They tend to see education as a series of isolated skills to be mastered. There is little or no connection to the real world of the child. The second school of thought considers the need for skills to be taught as the child makes connections with the real world. Children's interests become the basis for curriculum content, but the teacher's goals for needed educational outcomes are not sacrificed. Too many children, under traditional methods of instruction, did not and still do not learn to the upper limits of their potential. "If medicine resisted change and growth as strongly as education, it would still be using leeches" (Dr. Zelda Maggart, personal communication).

How the Past Informs the Present: Making Connections

The history of an integrated approach is indeed fragmented. There exist many examples of attempts to provide for children a learning environment to meet their developmental needs, follow their interests, and offer a curriculum both relevant and holistic in nature. Historically, the integrated approach existed as a total philosophy only in some areas of Britain which, for about twenty-five years, made a studied attempt to implement this kind of learning environment. The failure of attempts in the United States had to do less with actual theory and more to do with the implementation of that theory. A combination of inadequate teacher training, lack of parent involvement and understanding, and the lack of an overriding, comprehensive philosophical view contributed to this failure. The approach was viewed by many as a "methodology" or instructional strategy rather than a holistic view of the learning/teaching process.

History, as outlined in this chapter, supports an integrated approach. In addition, what we now know about how children develop and learn contraindicates the use of more traditional methods of education. However, to make the integrated approach work, we have learned that we cannot approach curriculum independent of theory and philosophy, the delivery of instruction without adequate training, and the use of multiage groups without a clear understanding of development. Parents need to be a part of the education process; they also need to understand that learning does not take place in a vacuum. Parents as well as teachers have to understand that young children learn through active participation with their environment, and that "play" is a critical component of learning.

What's Happening Now

The integrated approach, as described in this text, is practiced in individual classrooms across the country, often not in totality. Partial uses of the approach may be seen in the use of theme studies within same-age classrooms, or in the integration of certain content areas—most likely mathematics and science or language arts and social studies. In Santa Fe, New Mexico, the State Department of Education is encouraging more integration of subject matter. The Bureau of Indian Affairs is also encouraging teachers to look at more ways to integrate subject matter. Early childhood programs are focusing more on what is considered "developmentally appropriate curriculum," basing their decisions on the National Association for the Education of Young Children's "Developmentally Appropriate Practice" guidelines for the education of children from birth through grade three.

Currently, the major restructuring programs throughout the country are incorporating many of the aspects of the integrated approach. Included is the work and research of Howard Gardner, Ted Sizer, James Comer, and Henry Levin, as well as the research from the cooperative learning movement. Howard Gardner's (Harvard University) revolutionary research on intelligence disputes the traditional thinking about the superiority of linguistic and mathematical intelligence (*Frames of Mind* 1983, *The Unschooled*

Mind 1991, *Multiple Intelligences: The Theory in Practice* 1993). His theory of multiple intelligences tells us that we must be supportive of varying intel loctual strengths which encompass not only linguistic and mathematical intelligence, but also musical, spatial, bodily-kinesthetic and intra- and interpersonal intelligences. The traditional approaches to teaching do not encourage the child to develop all of the intelligences mentioned, and often hides abilities in children who do not excel in linguistic or mathematical achievement. Gardner's theory helps us to understand that children learn in different ways, according to their strengths. This requires an environment which offers many different kinds of materials and experiences so children can construct their own personal understanding of their world, guided by knowledgeable adults. The integrated approach not only allows children to experience their world from their own points of strength, but encompasses a curriculum that is rich in all of the intelligences. Beyond proposing a theory of multiple intelligences, Gardner also supports differing ways of teaching the curriculum, which, in turn, supports varying ways of learning.

As in England during the time of the Plowden Report, educational reform is a vital movement in the United States today. The incredible number of children who are failing in our schools has made it obvious that methods of education now in place must be carefully reexamined. One of the most carefully structured school reform movements is The Coalition of Essential Schools directed by Ted Sizer (Brown University). The Coalition of Essential Schools has developed guidelines which are understood as the nine basic principles of RE: Learning (Regarding learning). The nine principles include:

1. Intellectual focus. Children should learn to use their minds well.
2. Simple goals. Students should master a limited number of essential skills and areas of knowledge.
3. Universal goals. The school's goals should apply to all students.
4. Personalization. Teaching and learning should be personalized.
5. Student as worker. Students should be active learners while the teachers are the coaches.
6. Diploma by "exhibition." There should be a successful demonstration of mastery of skills and knowledge.
7. Tone. The school should stress values of unanxious expectation, of trust, and decency. Parents should be collaborators.
8. Staff. Principals and teachers should see themselves as generalists first and specialists second.
9. Budget. Emphasis should be on lowering the teacher/pupil ratio and time for collective staff planning and collaboration.

RE: Learning programs share certain characteristics which support what has been learned from the findings of the British primary school movement.

1. Students act as researchers; particular emphasis is placed on student-designed and executed projects. Multiple resources are available.
2. Teachers as coaches; they serve as resources, but challenge students to be responsible for their own discoveries.
3. Less emphasis is placed on lecture and more emphasis is placed on students working together on research projects.
4. Students demonstrate their proficiency and understanding of subject matter through actual exhibition of work.
5. "Less is more"; subject matter is explored in depth. The accumulation of unrelated facts is less important than the understanding of a major concept.
6. Less emphasis placed on standardized time frames; more emphasis on children learning according to their needs.
7. Less emphasis placed on right and wrong answers and standardized solutions. More emphasis on continued learning, divergent thinking, and problem solving.
8. Students are encouraged to believe that each individual should be treated with dignity and respect.
9. Education is seen as partnerships within the school and the surrounding community.

James Comer (Yale) focuses on the development of schools that foster positive social and academic climates. A major component of a Comer school is that all the stake holders in the educational process (principals, teachers, support staff, parents) are involved in the governance and management of the school. There is a policy that prohibits "blaming" one stake holder group for school failure. Emphasis is placed on understanding the problem or problems unique to a particular school, and solving them cooperatively. Emphasis also is placed on including mental health professionals as part of the governing team to ensure that the team is child-sensitive and relationship-sensitive. Schools modeled after Comer's philosophy tend to be seen as relaxed environments in which kids feel secure and interact with each other and staff easily. All of the teachers in the school accept responsibility for all of the children. Children feel cared about and teachers feel empowered. Schools become a place where people can connect emotionally, where expectations are high, and where children are helped to meet those expectations. The link between home and school is crucial, so that both parents and teachers send the same message to students about the importance of developing their potential.

The Comer model emphasizes the importance of parent/school relationships and demonstrates, as did the schools in Britain, that parent involvement is the key to school success. Empowerment of teachers and parents involvement in school governance were also recognized as critical factors in the success of the British primary schools.

The extensive research on cooperative, competitive, and individualistic approaches to learning indicate that cooperative learning experiences promote overall higher achievement than the other two approaches. These results hold true across age, subject, and task content.

The discussion process, inherent in cooperative models, promotes self-discovery and the development of higher-level cognitive strategies for task analysis. Opportunities for the sharing of ideas, problems, and their solutions help children to understand academic tasks as well as interpersonal issues from multiple perspectives.

The very nature of cooperative learning requires that children work together in groups. It is through these experiences that children are motivated to develop a sense of responsibility to and for others and to the attainment of the group's goals. Children in these groups tend to be more supportive of their peers, providing not only feedback and encouragement, but help in the creation of new ideas for their projects and tasks.

Considerations: A Summary of Our Thoughts

The integrated model described in this book is a combination of the highly successful British primary school research, and a synthesis of the current restructuring movement. It is an approach that supports a child-centered classroom with many opportunities for peer interactions. Problem-solving skills and the development of higher order thinking are cultivated and enhanced through work on projects that are thematic in nature. This approach is concerned with children becoming self-directed and socially responsible. Curriculum comes from the children's interests, guided by the teachers' objective or objectives for academic content. The involvement of parents as well as other professionals related to education is necessary for the success of the model.

Children growing up to live and work well into the twenty-first century need different kinds of educational experiences from those who were reaching adulthood in the early 1900s. Taking the best from a historically sound theory of learning and teaching and combining it with current research and perspectives on the learning process seems the logical thing to do!

Suggested Activities

1. Listening to Children

One of the most fruitful ways of finding out what children need from a learning environment is to ask them directly. Too often, we disregard the voices of children, not taking into consideration what they understand about themselves as intellectual, social, and emotional beings. Children do not always know how to articulate this knowledge; therefore it becomes even more important for the teacher to listen and elicit as much information as possible. It is important for a teacher to recognize that children are not always tactful in how they say things. It is easy for a teacher to become defensive and to protect his or her position of authority. When this happens, it becomes difficult to "hear" the meaning behind the children's words.

Whether you are a pre-service teacher or an in-service teacher, choose some children of varying ages and ask them the following questions:

1. What do you like best about school?
2. What activities do you most enjoy?
3. Do you have time to be with your friends?
4. Are you learning more ways to get along with your friends?
5. Do you think you are a good learner? What makes you think so?
6. How do you think you learn best?
7. What do you dislike about school?
8. What changes could be made so that you would like school better?

Below are some responses from children who were asked these questions by teachers and apprentice teachers.

What I like about school, by Jessica, age 11: "I like to work with my hands on stuff. I like building things, like bridges and castles. I get bored if the same thing is repeated over and over. I like working in groups. I like projects that let you express your feelings. My favorite project was making cornhusk dolls as part of our study of colonial America."

What I hate about school, by Rachel, age 10: "I hate school because it's not fun. Teachers should understand us better. We want to learn about things that are important and interesting to us. I'm afraid of all the fighting in school. I think kids fight because they're bored."

What I like about school, by Francesca, age 9: "I like it when kids get along and help each other with problems. I like it when we learn things through projects rather than textbooks. We do lots of things in our class that are fun and interesting and I learn a lot. In science, we made hot air balloons out of tissue paper."

What I hate about school, by Alexandria, age 11: "I hate history taught from textbooks. Textbooks deprive you of thinking. Learning is fun. Spelling is stupid and useless. I know I have to learn to spell, but rote memory and repeated writing of words is stupid. I don't like that kids in my class are not allowed to learn at their own pace. School pushes you forward or keeps you back."

What I like about school, by Jessie, age 12: "I like the way we learned about Egypt and the Middle Ages. We worked in groups and developed questions for other groups to answer. We got dressed up in costume and went on a hidden treasure hunt. We had to know lots of information about Egypt to find the treasure. I like reports that tell me what I'm doing well and where I need to improve. I like to solve problems and to make my own choices as to where I am going to do my work in the classroom. It's hard for me to sit still at a desk. In my room we can move around and use a variety of different resources to complete our work."

Compare the answers you receive from children to the answers we have chosen to print in this chapter. Is there a common theme? Do your children share the same concerns? How can you address some of the concerns your children raise? Is the school or district aware of children's concerns? Can you use your children's likes more effectively?

2. Readings to Broaden the Understanding

It is important to have a perspective of the influences, both historical and present, on educational restructuring. If you choose to adopt the integrated approach, in part or in total, it is important to understand and be in agreement with the overriding philosophy, and to recognize that this approach, in different forms, has been around for many years. The readings listed below are representative of past and present and have been chosen to inform the reader so that the chapters that follow can be interpreted and assimilated with more background.

Historical Perspectives

Dewey, John. (1938). *Experience and Education.* New York: MacMillan.

Goodlad, J. I., Anderson, Robert H. (1963). *The Nongraded Elementary School.* New York: Harcourt, Brace and World, Inc.

Holt, John. (1964). *How Children Fail.* New York: Pittman Publishing Corp.

James, Charity. (1972). *Young Lives at Stake.* New York: Agathon Press, Inc.

Kohl, Herbert. (1967). *36 Children.* New York: The New American Library, Inc.

Kozol, Jonathan. (1967). *Death at an Early Age.* Boston: Houghton Mifflin.

Silberman, Charles E. (1970) *Crisis in the Classroom.* New York: Random House.

There are a great number of books, now out of print, which were published during the 1960s about the British primary schools and the integrated day, particularly by Citation Press, New York. If any of these can still be found, they can be of great interest and value.

Some titles include:

Cook and Mack; *The Teacher's Role*
Cook and Mack; *The Pupil's Day*
Cook and Mack; *The Head Teacher's Role*
Dean; *Recording Children's Progress*
Featherstone; *An Introduction*
Grugeon and Grugeon; *An Infant School*
Kogan; *The Government of Education*
Palmer; *Space, Time and Grouping*
Pearson; *Trends in School Design*
Pidgeon; *Evaluation of Achievement*

These books were all a part of the Anglo-American Primary School Project, funded by the Ford Foundation and the (British) Schools Council.

Recent Perspectives

Allen, Jo Beth, and Mason, Janan M., eds. (1989). *Risk Makers, Risk Takers, Risk Breakers.* New Hampshire: Heinemann Educational Books.

Brendtro, Larry K., Brokenleg. Martin, Van Bockern, Steve. (1990). *Reclaiming Youth at Risk: Our Hope for the Future.* Indiana: National Education Service.

Jervis, Kathe and Montag, Carol, eds. (1991). *Progressive Education for the 1990s: Transforming Practice.* New York: Teachers College Press.

Kozol, Jonathan. (1991). *Savage Inequalities.* New York: Crown Publishers, Inc.

Gardner, Howard. (1983). *Frames of Mind.* New York: Basic Books.

Gardner, Howard. (1991). *The Unschooled Mind.* New York: Basic Books.

Gardner, Howard. (1993). *Multiple Intelligences: The Theory in Practice.* New York: Basic Books.

Miller, Ron. (1990). *What are Schools for? Holistic Education in American Culture.* Chapters 8 and 9. Vermont: Holistic Education Press.

Educational Leadership. Alexandria, VA: Association for Supervision and Curriculum Development. The major themes of particular issues of this journal are:

Restructuring Schools: What's Really Happening? (May 1991). *48* (8).
Building a Community for Learning. (September 1992) *50* (1).
Improving School Quality. (November 1992). *50* (3).
Authentic Learning. (April 1993). *50* (7).
The Changing Curriculum. (May 1993). *50* (8).

Kappan. Bloomington, Indiana: Phi Delta Kappa. Listed below are the lead topics of the particular issue of this journal:

Perspectives on the New American Schools Development Corp. (December 1992). *74* (4).
The Politics of Education Reform. (December 1993). *75* (4).
Future Schools. (January 1994). *75* (5).

Some questions to consider after reading:

What were the concerns of the 1960s "radical" education writers? How are those same concerns manifested today? What was done about them previously? What is being done today?

What "got lost" through the years of the original British Infant School model? Why did this happen? What indications are there that this model still exists in some form in the United States? Why did these "pieces" survive when the model itself did not?

What has prompted the current restructuring movement across the United States? Does this movement relate to past efforts in school reform? Is restructuring really taking hold today? If so, how and where? What is interfering with the implementation of change, especially if this change is a radical departure from the norm?

References

Blackie, John. (1971). *Inside the Primary School.* New York: Schocken Books.
Bredecamp, Sue, ed. (1987). *Developmentally Appropriate Practice in Early Childhood Programs: Serving Children from Birth Through Age 8.* Washington D.C.: National Association for the Education of Young Children.
Brown, Mary and Precious, Norman. (1968). *The Integrated Day in the Primary School.* London: Ward Lock Educational.
Dennison, George. (1969). *The Lives of Children.* New York: Random House.
Dewey, John. (1938). *Experience and Education.* New York: Collier Books.
Evans, Ellis D. (1975). *Contemporary Influences in Early Childhood Education.* New York: Holt, Rinehart and Winston, Inc.
Gardner, Howard. (1983). *Frames of Mind.* New York: Basic Books.

Gardner, Howard. (1991). *The Unschooled Mind*. New York: Basic Books.

Gardner, Howard. (1993). *Multiple Intelligences: The Theory in Practice*. New York: Basic Books.

Herndon, James. (1968). *The Way It Spozed to Be*. New York: Simon and Schuster.

Herndon, James. (1971). *How to Survive in Your Native Land*. New York: Simon and Schuster.

Holt, John. (1964). *How Children Fail*. New York: Pittman Publishing Corporation.

Humphreys, Allen H., Post, Thomas R. and Ellis, Arthur K. (1992). Developing Relationships among Mathematics and Other Topics: an Interdisciplinary Approach. In Thomas R. Post, ed. *Teaching mathematics in grades K-8*. (pp. 331–361). Massachusetts: Allyn Bacon.

Jacobs, Heidi Hayes, ed. (1989). *Interdisciplinary Curriculum, Design and Implementation*. Virginia: Association for Supervision and Curriculum Development.

Kohl, Herbert. (1967). *36 Children*. New York: New American Library, Inc.

Kozol, Jonathan. (1967). *Death at an Early Age*. Boston: Houghton Mifflin Company.

Children and Their Primary School: A Report of the Central Advisory Council for Education. (Plowden Report) (England). (1967). London: Her Majesty's Stationery Office.

Saylor, Galen J., Alexander, William M., and Lewis, Arthur J. (1981). *Curriculum Planning for Better Teaching and Learning*. New York: Holt, Rinehart and Winston.

The Importance of Developmental Theory in the Classroom

According to Erikson, an individual has neither a set personality nor a set character structure. A person is always a personality in the making; developing and redeveloping. His theory is best understood from the perspective of the life cycle. (Tribe, 1992, p. 5)

Development encompasses every aspect of a child's growth. As Erikson suggests, a person is always in the process of "forming." There are predictable patterns as to how the individual changes over time, but each is still an individual, moving at his or her own rate, and learning in his or her own way. The environment can be supportive of these changes and differences, assisting in the ongoing evolution of the person—physically, intellectually, socially, and emotionally. To be supportive, the environment must be appropriate, addressing the child's needs at any given time and being sensitive to these needs as they change.

A Window into Two Classrooms

Classroom 1: A Multi-Age Integrated Classroom of Children 8, 9, and 10 Years Old

Four children are sitting around a table with the teacher: two eight-year-olds, a nine-year-old and one ten-year-old. On the table are Cuisenaire rods, base ten blocks, chips of four colors from the chip trading game, beans and beansticks, several different kinds of mats including base ten mats, and chip trading tills as well as those mats created specifically by the teacher for beans and beansticks. These are all materials which can be used successfully to help children learn the concept of place value, and are especially helpful when this concept is needed to understand the skill of subtraction with regrouping.

The teacher has chosen these four children to work in a small group on the concept of three-digit subtraction with regrouping. Her choice of a work group has been determined from careful observation of the children, and careful listening to their discussions. The teacher was interested in putting a group of children together who socially were at basically the same level so that they could work cooperatively, easily negotiating their tasks without the distraction of major differences in social skills. She also wanted a group of children who indicated a readiness as well as a need for the use of the subtraction operation during project work. Satisfied with their basic understanding of the subtraction process as well as place value, she wishes to extend their ability to work with larger numbers. The project they are currently working on will require this skill. The teacher recognizes that for children at this developmental level, skill training still requires the manipulation of physical materials, and that the problem has to have relevance to what the child understands about his or her world. The teacher also knows that, cognitively, children at this stage of development are ready to begin to think about their thinking, becoming more aware of strategies and using these strategies more consciously. The teacher is also concerned with offering these children an opportunity to view a problem from more than one perspective, because she understands that this is an important developmental task for this age group.

The teacher poses a problem: "You know that Mr. Haley's class and ours are going to be decorating the hall for the estimation fair with balloons. If I have 325 balloons in this box, and Mr. Haley's class has volunteered to blow up 179 of them, how would I go about figuring out how many I had left for our class to inflate? You may work together as a group, or in pairs, and you may use any of the materials we have out on the table as well as paper and pencil. What is important is to keep track of how you worked out your answer, as I suspect that you will not all do it the same way. I will be asking you to explain your thinking! After you have worked out a solution, we will share our answers and discuss how we got them. That way, we can learn from each other and maybe find several ways to work out the same problem." The teacher then watches and listens carefully as the children set to work solving a real problem. (A full description of these mathematical manipulations can be found in a variety of current mathematics text books.)

Classroom 2: A Traditional Third Grade

The children are sitting at desks facing the teacher who is at the chalkboard. The children have been asked to open their math texts to a specific page dealing with word problems involving the subtraction of three-digit numbers.

"Eyes up here," the teachers states quietly but firmly. Twenty-five pairs of eyes look up almost simultaneously as the teacher continues her lesson. "You will need to pay particular attention to how to do these problems, as this is a hard topic to learn!" The teacher asks one of the children to read the first word problem. She then asks the children to state what the problem asks them to do. She calls on one child to write the problem on the board:

$$246 - \underline{157}$$

The teacher tells the children, "First, look at the ones column. Can we take 7 from 6?" A strong chorus of "No's" follows. "Right. So we must move over to the tens column, take one from there and regroup into the ones column. How many ones do we have now?" "16." "Yes, and how many tens left in the tens place?" "3." The "chorus" however is getting smaller and less vocal. "Can we take 7 from 16?" "yes—it's 9," answer several children.

The teacher proceeds to work through the next regrouping with hundreds and tens, asking the children to respond with each step. However, the numbers of children responding as well as any feeling of assurance that what is being said is correct keeps diminishing. By the time the problem is finished, two or three children are responding, with most of the rest either looking totally perplexed or off in space somewhere, not knowing what is going on. Knowing from experience that many of the children have not understood the process, the teacher "walks" the entire class through another example or two before assigning them the practice problems at the bottom of the page. Even before she turns to replace her teacher's edition on her desk, more than a dozen hands are in the air; children are asking for help! Since all children are expected to learn this material in the same way at the same time, there is no real opportunity to address individual differences in readiness. Children are not encouraged to increase social skills by working cooperatively together on problem solving, nor are they asked to consider that there might be more than one way to solve the problems. The lack of manipulatives and a relevant problem make the learning situation more abstract, taking it out of the concrete realm that children need in order to make a task important to them. It also removes the task from a situation in which children can choose materials and strategies to help them accomplish their goal.

The Integrated Classroom and Developmental Appropriateness

The classrooms described above demonstrate differences in how teachers view their classrooms, and in how teachers were trained to respond to individual differences in how children think and act. Most teachers are guided by curriculum, not children. In the integrated classroom, teachers are guided by developmental principles; curriculum becomes secondary to children. A developmentally appropriate classroom is one in which children's interests and particular ways of learning are considered in setting up the physical space and in choosing materials and instructional strategies. Developmental theory provides the teacher with a body of knowledge that helps him or her understand the ever-changing growth patterns of his or her students. The teacher makes decisions about groupings of children for specific tasks according to the children's social/emotional and academic levels. When the issue is the subordination of teaching to learning, the understanding of development is most crucial.

The success of an integrated classroom relies heavily on the teacher's knowledge of what is reasonable to expect from each student to ensure success both academically and socially. The classroom learning environment cannot be static; flexibility is the key component. The teacher must be willing to change direction with regard to the curriculum content and instructional strategies as children change through the developmental process. The teacher assesses how children use the classroom as a learning environment by determining not only what a child knows at any given time, but also what the child is in the process of knowing. For the teacher, this kind of classroom requires taking a perspective that clearly addresses the dynamic, ongoing process of matching the learning environment to the dynamic, ongoing process of children's development over time.

Traditionally, teachers primarily have been concerned only with the academic growth of the child. However, it is clear that the goal of education is to increase competency in all areas of human development (Hendrick, 1984). This approach takes into consideration the child as a complex human being, necessitating recognition of social, emotional, and physical growth needs as well as cognitive. For example, it is necessary to teach children coping skills because this is the ability that underlies self-esteem. Self-esteem is a significant factor for successful academic achievement. Children with poor self-esteem are less likely to engage actively in the learning process because they are unwilling to risk failure. It is difficult for children to learn if they are not willing to take risks, and if they see failure as a condemnation of themselves. Children who become successful learners are those children who also learn to take increasing responsibility for their own behavior. Developing a sense of control over themselves and their actions allows them to become more committed to their learning process (Collis and Dalton, 1990). In addition to issues of self-esteem and self-regulated behavior, the elementary school-age child is developing the social skills that assist him or her in becoming an accepted member of a peer group. The peer group is the mirror that reflects the image of self. If a child lacks the necessary skills for getting along socially, he or she will be left on the sidelines, affecting his or her overall sense of competency as well as his or her learning

The Study of Human Development

The study of human development is the study of how the individual changes over time. Human development looks at the cognitive, social, emotional, and physical aspects of the person as each aspect functions independently and in interaction with the others. It provides the knowledge base, which in turn provides the structure which enables the teacher to understand and make predictions about the child's behavior. The study of human development and the use of its principles in educating children is not haphazard, as it requires a body of scientific data based on a review of many individuals across populations and cultures. It encompasses a broad field which incorporates all those factors which influence the formation of the person evolving over the life cycle. The development of an individual follows a predictable pattern, but is often uneven. For instance, a child may be advanced cognitively for his or her age and yet be functioning at a less evolved social level. Environmental factors can affect the rate and quality of a child's development. For example, children who do not receive proper nutrition may, in fact, not reach their potential height. Children in learning environments which do not challenge intellectual curiosity may not reach their learning potential.

Human development is a field of study which enables us to evaluate such areas as the differences between the thought processes of a preschooler, an elementary school-age child, and an adolescent. Most developmental theorists use age ranges to describe a span of time in which certain changes in the child are most evident. For example, Piaget describes the ages between seven and eleven as "concrete operations." However, it is important to recognize that even within the specific age range noted, there may be considerable variation. The teacher uses developmental theory as a guide, remembering that each child is an individual, developing at his or her own rate. A child who is functioning significantly below what would be considered an expected behavior for his or her age range, may be subjected to factors that are negatively influencing the rate and quality of that child's development. A child who is significantly above what is considered the "norm" or expected behavior for an age range, may already be functioning at the next developmental level. In both cases, the teacher is responsive to where the child is in his or her own growth process, and will plan accordingly. A developmentally appropriate classroom is one in which all aspects of curriculum, room arrangement, and behavioral expectations are congruent with what the children in that classroom are capable of doing, given their present ability to understand the objects and events of their world.

Three Developmentalists: Piaget, Erikson, Vygotsky

These three developmentalists provide valuable information to the integrated classroom. Each theorist emphasizes a particular aspect of growth and development. When their theories are understood together, they provide an integrated framework for understanding the needs of the school-age child.

Jean Piaget (1896–1980): An Overview

Jean Piaget's legacy enables us to understand the differences of the child's thought processes from the adult's. His primary interest was epistemology—the study of the definition and the acquisition of knowledge. His theory is concerned with the development of "thinking" or "intelligence." For Piaget, intelligence is the individual's ability to adapt successfully to his or her social and physical environment (Overton, 1972). As a biologist, Piaget was concerned with the relationship of maturational changes *within* the individual and the effects of the environment *on* the individual. Piaget was not a maturationist in the true sense of the word, as he did not hold to the belief that certain behaviors were genetically predetermined to unfold naturally according to some inner time table (Crain, 1992). Piaget was really an interactionist, taking the position that genetics affected development in two ways. First, in all individuals, there is a biological drive to survive which requires adapting to and organizing the environment. Second, the individual comes into the world with certain innate reflexes which allow the newborn to begin exploring and interacting with the environment, thereby constructing an understanding of the objects and events in that environment. It is this continued interaction between the individual and the environment that underlies Piaget's theory.

Piaget's Concept of Cognitive Structures
Central to Piaget's theory is the concept of psychological structures or stable organizational patterns of behavior. It is through these structures that the individual understands his world. Structures, therefore, can be viewed as rules which are applied systematically. The extent to which these structures exist and are interrelated limit the child's understanding of the world at any given time. Structures develop as the individual's use of reflexes become modified into integrated wholes.

Assimilation and Accommodation
Piaget believed that inherent in the human being is a tendency to want to maintain a sense of internal balance or a state of equilibrium. As a child interacts with the environment, this balance is disturbed each time the understanding of the world is challenged. The child will actively seek to

regain a sense of internal balance through what Piaget terms *assimilation* and *accommodation*. These are the biological tendencies which serve the individual in his or her attempts to adapt to an ever-changing environment.

Assimilation is the process of taking in objects and events as they are. For example, a newborn will put everything in his or her mouth. He or she develops what Piaget calls a schema or an internal sensorimotor representation of the object or event which allows for generalization by repetition in similar or analogous circumstances (Piaget and Inhelder, 1969). When new information fits this existing schema, there is no "disequilibrium"; if the new information cannot be assimilated into existing schemas without some modifications, the process of accommodation occurs. The individual fits the new information in with the old, changing his or her schema and, therefore, his or her understanding of the world. These two processes, assimilation and accommodation, work together in the service of adaptation. Although assimilation can occur without accommodation, accommodation only occurs along with assimilation.

Piaget did not believe there was an objective, absolute reality that every child learns. He believed that through the processes of assimilation and accommodation each individual constructs his or her own reality by organizing and understanding experiences in meaningful ways that fit within existing knowledge. An example would be a young child who initially learns that the four-legged furry animal in his house is called a dog. He then proceeds to call all four-legged furry animals "dogs." On a trip to the zoo, the child sees a four-legged animal that does not have fur. His schema of four-legged animals is now challenged. In order to adapt to the reality that not all four-legged creatures are "dogs" or have fur, he must accommodate the new information into his existing schema. He now finds that there are four-legged animals called armadillos as well as dogs. Through this interaction with his environment, the child constructs his understanding of the animal world. Through the process of assimilation and accommodation, new structures or "rules" about animals develop. For learning to take place and for reality to shift, "cognitive conflict" must occur—the challenging of a present way of knowing with a newly modified understanding as the result.

Piaget's Conception of Knowledge

Piaget conceived of knowledge as a *process*. To know something required action—physical, mental, or both. Initially, all knowledge is constructed by direct physical contact with objects or events. For a young child, to know a ball is to pick it up, put it in his or her mouth, feel it. As the child matures, he or she can mentally act on objects through the use of mental images and symbols. The progressive disassociation of schemas from overt activity, and the further interrelation of schemas into more complex systems, allows for thinking about the world and ultimately "thinking about thinking"

(Overton, 1972, p. 92). According to Piaget, knowledge was a process or repertoire of actions rather than an inventory of stored information (Thomas, 1992).

Piaget's Stage Theory
Stage 1: sensorimotor: birth to 2 years

Infants begin to engage in rudimentary classification, organizing physical action schemas such as sucking and grasping, and learning about objects and others as separate from self and permanent in time and space.

Stage 2: preoperational thought: 2 to 7 years

Thinking is unsystematic and illogical, based on perception and the child's perspective of the world. Symbols and internal images allow the child to think about things that are not in his or her immediate environment. Language becomes more developed, allowing for shared communication.

Stage 3: concrete operations: 7 to 11 years

Children develop the ability to think systematically, classifying and ordering the world in more logical sequences, still dependent on concrete objects and activities for understanding.

Stage 4: formal operations: 11 to adulthood

Thinking now is more abstract, symbols do not have to be related to concrete objects or events, and hypothetical reasoning becomes more possible.

Piaget is considered a stage theorist. Although the individual is always in the process of changing, there are certain periods or stages in the growth cycle which can be characterized by qualitatively different thought. Each stage is usually studied as if it were a static point on the growth continuum; however, it is important to acknowledge that there is always movement within each stage. Each stage, therefore, contains the seeds of the next stage and incorporates the previous stage. Stages are normally considered invariant, which means that every individual will move through the stages in the same sequence. In reality, there are differences between individuals as to the pace at which they move through these stages and the quality of the movement. Theorists such as Piaget associated ages or age ranges with stages as guidelines for prediction. Piaget, however, was less interested in assigned ages than in the increasingly complex ways that an individual thinks about his or her world (Crain, 1992).

Sensorimotor Stage: Birth to 2 Years
In Piaget's first stage, the infant/toddler develops a rudimentary classification system in his or her initial attempt to organize his or her world. Through experiences such as touching, banging, mouthing, and grasping

objects, he or she learns that objects have a form of their own, that they exist separate from his or her own action, and that they are permanent in space and time (Thomas, 1992). The child begins to appreciate that he or she can act on the environment and affect outcomes. During this time period, the child develops symbolic activity. For instance, a child may begin to use an object such as a block to represent another object, such as a car. At the end of this stage, the child begins to assign words to objects and events, and can now remember an event and imitate it in play, such as his mother bathing his baby sibling.

Preoperational Thought: 2 to 7 Years

The child entering into the second stage has already begun to use language as a way of communicating and representing his or her world. Language in this stage tends to be egocentric in that the child assumes that everyone else sees the world as he or she does, making it necessary for the adult to use language that reflects the child's point of view. The child during this stage now can relive the past and anticipate the future. Thoughts and speech are still basically disconnected, precluding logical association and continuous thought processes (Thomas, 1992). Because the child's thinking is still basically unsystematic and illogical, he or she is not able to perceive accurately relationships between objects and events. The child cannot perform operations in his or her mind. *Operations* are actions that are internalized, reversible, and coordinated into systems that have laws that apply to the entire system and not just a single operation. The child during this stage has not yet developed the mental structures required for consistent application of a "rule." Classification is haphazard. The child relies on the senses: seeing is believing. For example, the preoperational child will choose to take four pennies over a nickel because it *looks* like more. It is also difficult for a child in this stage to think of events as continuous. Each event appears as a still photograph with the logical connections missing. Because the child in this stage focuses on one dimension of an object or event, he or she cannot *conserve*. *Conservation* requires the understanding that an amount is not affected by changes in shape or placement.

The child in this stage struggles with issues related to the constancy of identity. Halloween masks transform the wearer into what or who the costume represents. The child of this age is very literal. For instance, the teacher who informs a child that his mother is going to be late picking him up because she is tied up at the office conjures up images for the child of his or her mother being physically tied to a desk or a chair.

Social thinking parallels scientific thinking. The child's ability to understand the social world is limited by the same cognitive structures that govern his or her understanding of objects, events, and relationships. The preoperational child has difficulty considering more than one perspective at a time, relying on perception as the basis for decision making. For instance, when mother comes home tired and flops on the sofa, a preoperational child may bring her favorite blanket and doll to her mother. This is what the mother would do for the child if she were tired. It is beyond the child's social thinking to take the perspective of the mother who really would like to be left alone with a good mystery novel and an iced tea. Piaget believed that peers are more important than adults for imparting social perspective. Peers are more likely to force accommodation than adults, who tend not to dispute how the child sees the world. Children tend to engage in more conflict with peers than with adults, and this offers more opportunities for viewpoints to be challenged (Crain, 1992).

Between the ages of 4 and 7, children go through what Piaget described as a substage of the preoperational period. He called this substage *intuitive thought*. During this time, the child begins to question the absoluteness of his or her perceptions. Prior to the onset of intuitive thought, if a child is shown two balls of exactly the same amount of clay, he or she will acknowledge that they are the same. When one ball is then rolled into a hot dog shape and is compared again to the second ball, the child will respond that the hot dog shape is bigger. The child is relying strictly on his or her perception of what *looks* like more or "bigger," completely disregarding the logic that no clay had been added or taken away.

As the child comes closer to the end of this stage, he or she becomes less reliant on perception alone and more reliant on some initial intuitive logic. He or she is beginning to do what Piaget calls *conserve*. *Conservation* is a gradual intellectual process that moves the child from this transitional stage to the next stage, concrete operations.

Concrete Operations and Conservation: 7 to 11 Years
By the time the child is in this stage, he or she is able to hold in his or her mind two attributes of an object or event at the same time. For example, a child presented with two identical glasses of liquid, who watches the examiner pour one of the glasses into a taller, thinner glass, can now say with assurance that nothing was added, nothing was taken away, and that therefore the amount of liquid in the original glass and the amount of liquid in the taller thinner glass is equal, *despite* appearances. Piaget called this *conservation of substances*. Children learn to conserve number, length, substance (liquid and solid), area, weight, solid volume, and displaced volume at different times during this stage (Labinowicz, 1980).

Conservation tasks before and after transformations.   Children watch throughout the transformations, with the experimenter asking specific questions to determine if the child can conserve in that area.

Number: The child is asked if there are the same number of pennies in each row.

The pennies in one row are then moved close together and the child is asked again if there are the same number of pennies in each row, or if one row has more.

Length: Two sticks of equal length are placed parallel and the child is asked if each of the sticks is as long as the other.

Then, one stick is moved so that one stick extends well past the other. The child is again asked if the sticks are of equal length or if one is longer.

Liquid: Two glasses that are the same size and shape are filled with the exact same amount of water. The child is asked if there is the same amount of water in each glass.

One of the glasses is replaced by a shorter, fatter glass. The water from the glass which has been removed is now poured into the new, empty glass, and the child is asked if the glasses hold the same amount of water, or if one has more.

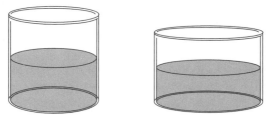

Mass: The child is presented with two equal balls of clay and asked if there is the same amount of clay in each ball.

One ball of clay is rolled into a hot dog or sausage shape. The child is now asked if each piece has the same amount of clay, or if one has more.

Area: The child is presented with two pieces of green paper, which represent grass, on each of which is placed a cow or other farm animal. Four identical paper houses are added to each "scene," placed close together on each paper. Then the child is asked if each cow has the same amount of grass to eat and the same amount of area to roam.

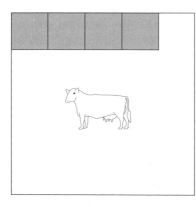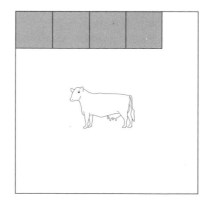

The houses on one piece of paper are then spread around the cow, and the child is asked again if each cow still has the same amount of grass to eat, or if one cow has more.

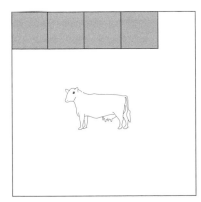 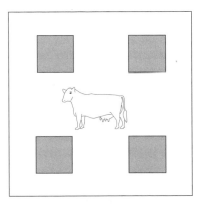

Weight: Two equal balls of clay are placed on a scale. The child is asked if the two balls of clay weigh the same amount. One ball of clay is flattened, and now, without placing the clay back on the scale, the child is asked if the two pieces of clay weigh the same, or if one weighs more.

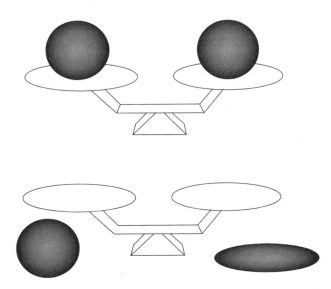

Volume: The child is asked if two balls of equal size and shape are dropped into two glasses of the same amount of water, will the water level rise equally in each glass? The examiner then drops the balls of clay into the glasses so that the child can see that the water levels are the same.

One piece of clay is removed from the water and reshaped, and the child is asked again if the water levels will rise equally, or if one will rise more.

How do all these conservation tasks inform the teacher? One specific example that is crucial to children's understanding of basic mathematical thinking, and especially the operations of arithmetic (adding, subtracting, multiplying, and dividing) is conservation of number. If a child still believes that five is five only when the five pennies are situated close together and that there are more if the row is stretched out, then this child cannot understand that every time you put two objects and three objects together you have a total of five objects, *always*. For the nonconserver, changing the *formation* of the quantity changes the quantity. It is this underlying sense of "numberness" that school beginners must have before they in any way can be successful with mathematical understanding and the operations of arithmetic which are a major focus of the primary grades. The teacher who does not have knowledge of Piaget's theory may require a child to do the written arithmetic without the necessary cognitive scaffolding. The child may be able to memorize facts, but not have the understanding to apply these concepts from one situation to another.

Although the child, in concrete operations, still requires extensive and varied experiences with concrete objects and events, he or she can now "operate" on these objects and events in his or her mind without the physical involvement characteristic of the preoperational stage. This detachment from physical action is only possible if the child's prior experience has included action-oriented learning. This means that during the preoperational stage, children must have many opportunities to learn about objects and events through all of their senses. For example, the preoperational child needs to have experiences filling, emptying, and "measuring" both wet and dry materials such as water and sand, before actual work with measurement can take place successfully. In addition, extensive experience with block building gives the needed scaffolding for future work with visual/spatial activities such as building models to accompany projects, learning space/size relationships, reading and making maps. Experimenting and exploring with a variety of physical materials provide children with a mental framework that becomes available for later planning and execution of ideas when physical materials are not necessarily present for the child to actively use during the planning stage.

The concrete operational child basically is still not able to relate to abstract symbols, such as algebraic equations. However, this is the age range during which learning the symbol systems of the culture is emphasized and reading, writing, and written arithmetic are primary focuses of the curriculum. For the child to understand the culture's symbol systems, learning has to take place in context, where symbols are used in meaningful ways to represent real life problems and events.

During the period of concrete operations, the child's language becomes "socialized." Unlike like the preoperational child's egocentric speech, the child now can communicate with an understanding of how language is used as a shared system. It is important to recognize that during this period, the child also develops the ability to hold two ideas in his or her head at one time, enabling him or her to think about his or her own perspective as well as those of others. While the preoperational child can seriate successfully only about three items, the concrete operational child can seriate an entire set of ten different length blocks according to relative dimensions such as size and length in an organized manner. The child can also think in terms of hierarchies. For example, a rose is a subset of a larger set, flowers. Berk (1991) describes a Piagetian class inclusion problem where preoperational children were shown 16 flowers, 4 of which were blue and 12 of which were yellow. When asked whether there were more "yellow flowers" or more "flowers," children at this stage responded that there were more yellow flowers. They failed to take into account the fact that both yellow and blue flowers were embedded in the superordinate category of "flowers."

Formal Operations: 11 Years to Adulthood

Prior to formal operations, children's thinking is limited to tangible objects that can be subjected to real activity. The stage of formal operations allows the individual to deal with hypothetical and abstract concepts. The adolescent is capable of examining varied possibilities to solutions to problems in his or her mind. Adolescents are able to project outcomes and compare and contrast the variables involved. Algebra and geometry can be thought about without the necessity of concrete materials. As with the concrete operational child, the child at formal operations also needs to have experienced the proper scaffolding during the previous stages in order to engage in abstract thought. Subjects such as algebra and geometry can become a form of mental gymnastics in which symbols are played with and the individual develops a sense of underlying patterns and structures.

Piaget acknowledged that maturation of the nervous system is critical in the attainment of different stages of thought. Assuming the individual has no physiological impairments, it is possible for him or her to achieve formal operations. Not all individuals, however, reach this stage of development because of inappropriate, limited, or nonexistent scaffolding. This reinforces the importance of appropriate learning environments. Children may be at somewhat different stages for different cognitive functions, such as social reasoning vs. scientific reasoning. However, Piaget believed that there was substantial unity in performances at each particular period (Crain, 1992).

For those teachers working with elementary school-age children, or anyone contemplating work with this age child, a more detailed investigation of Piaget's theory is encouraged. Refer to the suggested reading section at the end of this chapter for further readings.

Erik Erikson (1902–?): An Overview

While Piaget was concerned with the cognitive stages of development, Erikson's concern and interest was in the developmental changes regarding the child's relationship to his or her social and emotional world. His theory is based on the individual's successful resolution of specific conflicts that arise as the maturing ego and the social world interact. For each stage, Erikson described polarities, recognizing that a healthy ego is one in which there develops a balance between these opposite poles. Because of this, all stages in Erikson's theory have the word *versus* as part of the description, signifying the pull between two opposite positions. For Erikson, the human being is always in the process of "becoming." Conflicts that are descriptive of a stage continue through life, but are most pronounced during a particular time period. Although Erikson's theory continues past childhood and adolescence, the focus in this chapter will be on those stages that affect the elementary school-age child.

Erikson's Stage Theory
Stage 1: Trust versus mistrust: birth through 1 year

Stage 2: Autonomy versus doubt and shame: 1 to 3 years

Stage 3: Initiative versus guilt: 3 to 6 years

Stage 4: Industry versus inferiority: 6 years to puberty

Stage 5: Identity versus role confusion: adolescence

Stage theory posits that each new stage incorporates the stages that came before. Although each stage of Erikson's theory has a central theme, each stage resolution comes in part from the resolution of the prior stage. How a prior stage is resolved determines how the individual will approach the next stage.

Trust vs. Mistrust: Birth Through 1 Year

This initial stage focuses on the child's developing sense that his or her environment offers predictability, consistency, and reliability through experience with his or her caregiver. The beginnings of self-trust are developed, which means that the child is confident that he or she will get his or her needs met. Although the methods are not sophisticated, the child learns that through certain behaviors he or she can make the caregiver appear. The child also becomes aware that needs are not always met immediately and sometimes gratification must be delayed. Although it is necessary that the child become discriminating in his or her trust, Erikson states that without hope that comes from trust, a child cannot move into the world ready and able to accept new challenges (Erikson, 1982, p. 60).

Autonomy vs. Doubt and Shame: 1 to 3 Years

As the child develops, he or she becomes aware of his or her own separateness from others. For the young child, this stage is very much a stage of saying "no," even when complying with adults' wishes. The constant no-saying is a way for the child to say that he or she exists and has control over what happens to him or her. The "I am" and "I can" of this stage is balanced by the growing requests of adults in the child's life to conform to certain societal expectations.

From this stage comes the beginning of adjusting one's own needs to those of the larger society. This balance between independence and social regulation is necessary for self-determination and recognition of one's own will as well as the will of others (Crain, 1992). The doubt characteristic of this stage comes from the knowledge that one cannot always be in control, and the shame of not always looking good in other people's eyes.

Initiative vs. Guilt: 3 to 6 Years

The focus of this stage is mastery, balanced by adherence to limits that require knowing when one has gone too far to get something that is desired. It is a time of experimentation, with a strong need to test the affect one has on the environment. For the child, process is more important than product, yet behavior is goal-directed with specific plans and activities to accomplish those goals. At this stage, the child begins to develop a conscience and demonstrate self-regulated behavior. The danger is that adults often demand that the child exert more self-control than the child is capable of, leading to feelings of guilt when he or she cannot succeed. This is a time for make-believe play. Children learn about societal roles and relationships through play; by making believe they are mother or father, nurse or policeman, children gain insight into what they may become.

Industry vs. Inferiority: 6 Years to Puberty

Unlike the previous stage in which process is most important, the child at this stage is now interested in achieving a particular outcome. There develops through this stage a sense of purpose and accomplishment. During this stage for the child to develop a true sense of competency, accomplishments must be real and relevant. Although the child needs to balance feelings of competency with a realistic sense of what he or she can achieve, feelings of failure or inadequacy can feed a negative sense of self that prohibits the school-age child from adequately learning academic subject matter.

Identity vs. Role Confusion: Adolescence

The adolescent is discovering how he or she fits into the social world, and struggles with all the options of who he or she is and who he or she can become. For the adolescent, the discovery and adherence to his or her own values may mean alienation from family and friends. Because of the overwhelming nature of the choices and decisions facing the adolescent, many "drop out" or enter what Erikson terms a "psychological moratorium" in which the adolescent delays taking on adult commitments (Seifert and Hoffnung, 1991).

A classroom actively supporting the healthy resolution of the central themes of stages 3 and 4 will provide experiences in which children can utilize play as a mechanism for learning about self, others, and role relationships. With younger children, the emphasis should be on the *process* of doing. It is the mastery of objects and events that provides the child with a sense of control over his or her environment, and the belief that he or she can be in charge of outcomes. Clear and consistent boundaries enable the child to experience and experiment with his or her environment, and at the same time develop the ability to self-regulate behavior. As the child moves into the fourth stage, more emphasis should be placed on the actual outcome, although process is still important. Because the child is concerned with achieving, comparisons to peers become more evident and can become negative, ultimately effecting the child's growing sense of self as competent. Feelings of adequacy are protected in children who are helped to recognize that "failure" is part of the learning process, and success is on a continuum which changes as the child develops and matures in both the social and academic realms.

Lev Vygotsky (1896–1934): An Overview

In contrast to Piaget, Vygotsky does not take the position that the child "constructs" knowledge through an initiation of activity by which he or she formulates his or her own reality. Vygotsky believed that although the child gains knowledge on his or her own, the avenue by which knowledge is acquired is cultural transmission. The child learns about the world by interacting with adults and older peers around objects or tools. For the young child, a trip to the supermarket with a parent who describes what is being selected and how it will be used becomes an experience in learning words for objects that are then categorized as food. These words carry various connotations according to the culture. The words and the connotations will change from culture to culture, but in all cases, experience itself will provide the child with the necessary language. Through this interaction with a knowledgeable adult, the child develops language, which becomes the content for thought.

The Development of Thought

Initially, speech is external, directing the child's activities and interactions. Developmentally, a child of 2 years will engage in outer speech, referencing absent objects learned through interactions with others. By 3 years, children can use self-guided speech, which enables the child to solve problems and plan. Although such outer speech may be characterized as "egocentric," this type of speech serves a different function for Vygotsky than for Piaget. Gradually, language becomes internalized, and by the time a child reaches 6 years, he or she uses less "outer," self-directed speech. By age 8, speech is fairly well internalized, guiding all forms of behavior required for cognitive problem solving as well as self-regulation of behavior in the social/emotional domain (Crain, 1992). Speech still directs activity, but it is now "inner speech." However, it should be noted that children of school age still frequently talk to themselves, as if their mouths are telling their hands what to do. This is normal developmental behavior, which is most frequently seen when a child is learning a new skill or engaging in a task that requires a sequential set of steps for accomplishment. This "self-talk" assists children in organizing their thinking when the steps necessary to perform the new skill become more internalized, the self-talk also becomes more internalized. In the integrated classroom, children are not expected to be quiet, so self-talk can be a natural part of learning. In the traditional classroom, where quiet is expected, this important learning strategy is often not permitted.

The Content of Knowledge

For Vygotsky, culture dictates knowledge. Language is the mental tool which enables the individual to use mental functions such as memory. When humans use signs as symbols, they engage in what is termed *mediated behavior*. In other words, they act out reality and alter it by using their capability for language to think and plan. Vygotsky believed that abstract thought required instruction in abstract sign systems such as writing and mathematics. He also made a distinction between scientific and spontaneous concepts. While spontaneous concepts come from the child's own experiences with the world, scientific concepts provide children with broader frameworks in which to understand their own spontaneous concepts (Crain, 1992).

Zone of Proximal Development

Vygotsky believed that developmental processes did not coincide with learning processes. Properly organized learning results in mental development.

> *The developmental process lags behind the learning process; this sequence then results in the zone of proximal development. Our analysis alters the traditional view that, at the moment a child assimilates the meaning of a word, or masters an operation such as addition or written language, her developmental processes are basically completed. In fact, they have only just begun at that moment. (Cole, Michael, John-Steiner, Vera, Scribner, Sylvia and Souberman, Ellen, eds. 1978, p. 90)*

The zone of proximal development is a way in which the teacher can assess not just what the child knows, but also what the child is in the process of knowing. The zone of proximal development defines those functions that have not yet matured but are in the process of maturing.

> *(The zone) is the distance between the actual developmental level as determined by independent problem solving, and the level of potential development as determined through problem solving under adult guidance or in collaboration with more capable peers. (Cole et al., 1978, p. 86)*

Let us return, briefly, to the four children working on subtraction with their teacher at the beginning of the chapter. First of all, notice that the teacher had chosen several manipulative materials for the children to use: beans and beansticks, Cuisenaire rods, and colored chips from the chip trading games. She had also put out place value mats whose columns reflected the material to be used. The problem the children were to solve was 325 minus 179. One child who started with Base Ten Blocks put out thirty-two orange rods in the tens column, then quickly removed a ten block and replaced it with ten white rods in the units place. He then proceeded to physically remove seventeen orange rods (tens) and nine white rods (ones), carefully noting that what was remaining on the mat was a total of 146 (fourteen orange rods and six white ones) even though he did not trade back ten orange rods for one square. The teacher asked him why he started with thirty-two orange rods and nineteen white rods rather than three squares (hundred blocks), two orange rods (tens) and nine white rods (ones). The child replied that he knew right away that he would need to "trade down" in order to "take away" the right number of tens and ones. The teacher gave this child another problem to do, similar to the first one, and asked him to tell her exactly what he was doing as he went along. The child did not make the trades initially that he had previously. Instead he went step by step, starting with the hundred squares and trading only what he needed for that step and subsequent ones. It was evident to the teacher that this child was in the process of knowing a "shortcut" to the process of subtraction with regrouping, but was not able to sustain the mental picture he had initially of needing to make these "trade downs" ahead of time when faced with a new problem. The teacher provided scaffolding in the form of questions, as well as asking for a demonstration of his previous approach. This enabled the child to recognize his former strategy and reapply it to a third problem that the teacher posed.

Thinking about Thinking

Metacognition is the process of thinking about one's own thinking. Metacognitive activities help the individual exercise some control over his or her mental processes. Metacognition allows the individual to develop a greater awareness of those strategies that enable him or her to approach a task successfully. Although Vygotsky did not use the term *metacognition*, he was interested in such things as the child's use of memory aids as a method of control over thought processes (Crain, 1992). His investigation into this process has been helpful in understanding the various mental strategies a child can consciously employ to complete a task.

Metacognitive strategies act as an "executor." The person using metaconitive strategies surveys the task at hand and then thinks about the most effective approach for that task. For example, a particular child attempting to learn a body of information may know that, for him, the most effective strategy is to read the material first, and then summarize what he has read by writing a paragraph or two in his notebook. Another child also uses the metacognitive function to accomplish the same task, but recognizes that, for her, outlining the information as she goes along is more efficient. One way to help children recognize the metacognitive process is to ask them to talk out loud as they go about determining how to tackle a problem. The teacher can feed back to the child information that the child has communicated about his or her approach and strategy choices. The more aware the child becomes of thinking about thinking, the more he or she can use this higher order function productively.

Conclusions on the Developmentalists

Piaget, Erikson and Vygotsky all provide understanding of children's perspectives of themselves and their relationships to the real world. These theories help to inform us of how the child gradually learns to understand objects and events as the child attempts to organize and make sense out of his or her experience. These theories also provide guidelines that can assist the teacher in predicting how an individual child understands him- or herself in relation to his or her social environment, and how the development of the self relates to interactions with an ever-expanding, larger world. For the elementary school-age child, the foundations for intellectual growth are established not just by changes in internal structures (Piaget), or the internalization of meaning through language (Vygotsky), but by also the development of a sense of personal trust, initiative, and competency (Erikson). Although each child enters the school community at a different point in the developmental process, the classroom environment can be supportive or nonsupportive of continued positive growth.

Howard Gardner, Theory of Multiple Intelligences: An Overview

Howard Gardner (1991) states that Piaget is indeed worthy of study because he is, beyond question, the single dominant thinker in his field. He goes on to say that in light of current understanding of human cognitive development, there are four particularly problematic aspects of Piagetian theory. First, there is the basic belief that development consists of a series of qualitative shifts in representation and understanding. Gardner suggests that many basic understandings are present at birth or shortly thereafter and do not undergo a lengthy developmental process as Piaget posited. The second problem that Gardner identifies is that developmental domains appear to be far more independent of one another than Piaget had believed. The structures of the mind are apparently able to evolve in different directions at different rates. Third, Piaget seemed to believe that the understanding of numbers lay at the center of the intellect. Gardner refutes the notion that logical-mathematical intelligence is the basis for all intellectual reasoning. And lastly, Gardner argues that Piaget made a fundamental error in his contention that an older child's more evolved ways of knowing erase earlier forms of knowing the world.

> *For the most part, children's earliest conceptions and misconceptions endure through the school era. And once the youth has left a scholastic setting, these earlier views of the world may well emerge (or reemerge) in full blown form. Rather than being eradicated or transformed, they simply travel underground; like repressed memories of early childhood, they reassert themselves in settings where they seem to be appropriate."* (Gardner, 1991, p. 29)

Gardner, while acknowledging Piaget's significant contribution to cognitive theory, clearly saw limitations to the way in which Piaget used logical-mathematical reasoning as central to the development of intelligence. Gardner's Theory of Multiple Intelligences suggests that there are at least seven intelligences, with each one being as important and vital to intellectual development as the other. Gardner posits, in addition to linguistic and logical-mathematical intelligence, that there exists a bodily-kinesthetic intelligence, two personal intelligences termed *inter*personal and *intra*personal, musical intelligence, and spatial intelligence. Gardner severely faults the traditional IQ tests, not for social bias, but for the fact that they test only the linguistic and logical-mathematical intelligences. He describes his theory as one that is based on a radically different idea of intelligence, which then projects a different way of looking at schools. Gardner sees an expanded view of intelligence, intelligences really, which support the idea that individuals are indeed unique, with different strengths and differing ways of learning and knowing. This viewpoint implies that schools must be personally and individually rather than collectively oriented.

One of the key elements of Gardner's theory is the idea that each intelligence may work independently of the others, and that the ability to be a "critical thinker" within one intelligence may not serve that person well in another intelligence. In other words, each of the intelligences has its own way of functioning; thus, the current wave of emphasis on "critical thinking skills," while important, needs to be considered in light of each of the posited intelligences, rather than through a blanket approach.

Gardner defines intelligence as "the ability to solve problems or fashion products that are of consequence in a particular cultural setting or community." He goes on to state that the "problem-solving skill allows one to approach a situation in which a goal is to be obtained and to locate the appropriate route to that goal." Creating a "cultural product is crucial to such functions as capturing and transmitting knowledge or expressing one's views or feelings." Gardner finishes his definition by describing "the problems to be solved range from creating an end for a story to anticipating a mating move in chess to repairing a quilt. Products range from scientific theories to musical compositions to successful political campaigns." (Gardner, 1993, p. 15)

Gardner also states that "Multiple intelligence theory is framed in light of the biological origins of each problem-solving skill." This means that only those skills or abilities universal to human beings are considered, and that, even with this "biological proclivity" for problem-solving, there must be "cultural nurturing of that domain." As an example he cites that, "language, a universal skill, may manifest itself as writing in one culture, as oratory in another culture, and as the secret language of anagrams in a third." (Gardner, 1993 p. 16) For those interested in the biological "roots" of each intelligence, as well as a detailed description of each intelligence, we encourage the reading of *Frames of Mind* (Gardner, 1985).

In brief, each of the intelligences can be described as follows:

Bodily-kinesthetic intelligence: The ability to use one's body in highly skilled ways, and to have mastery of the motions of the body. Examples would be a dancer, an athlete, a surgeon, and a mechanic.

Interpersonal intelligence: The ability to understand and "read" others' behaviors, feelings, and motivations; the ability to understand moods and temperaments and to deal effectively with them. Counselors, teachers, religious and spiritual leaders, an effective politician, and parents all belong in this category.

Intrapersonal intelligence: The ability to know oneself, one's feelings, moods, and motivations. Having this ability helps the individual to draw on them to help guide and understand his or her behavior.

Linguistic intelligence: The "word spinner"—one who has a sensitivity to the meaning of words, their sounds, inflections, and rhythms, as well as the ability to persuade through words—written or oral. This intelligence includes the capacity to use language as a means of instruction and recall. Poets, writers, political leaders, teachers, and lawyers all possess considerable linguistic intelligence.

Logical-mathematical intelligence: This intelligence involves the ability to reason abstractly and to order and reorder quantitatively, as well as the ability to recognize and solve significant problems. This category includes logicians, mathematicians, scientists, and lawyers.

Musical intelligence: The ability to hear and use pitch that is rhythmically arranged, as well as to use such pitch sequences to communicate with others. Examples are musicians (performers), composers, and listeners.

Spatial intelligence: The ability to create accurate mental images and to see the visual world as it is; the ability to create and recreate visual forms. The painter, the sculptor, even mathematicians and scientists are examples of this intelligence.

We cannot urge the reader strongly enough to indulge in the careful study of *Frames of Mind*. This short overview does not do justice to the important contribution this theory makes to the understanding of intelligence.

Gardner's Stages of Development

In *Multiple Intelligences: The Theory in Practice,* (Gardner, 1993), Gardner extends his theory of intelligences to include a vision of school vastly different from the average school of today. Building on his research with children of various ages over the past decade, he suggests a theory of three stages of cognitive development that can more clearly meet the needs of multiple intelligences for school-age children. For the young child to about age 7, the physical environment and learning experiences should resemble the children's museum, an unusual educational setting being developed across the country. Children's museums are designed to be exploratory and interactive. Children's museums offer a wide variety of activities that allow children to experience, experiment, and try things out within each of the intelligences, always with and under the guidance of knowledgeable adults and differently advanced peers. The Children's Museum in Santa Fe, New Mexico, rotates its exhibits, providing many opportunities for children to interact with animals, creative materials, science experiments, physical activities, and culturally relevant projects. Examples of these exhibits would include a corn snake and a cockroach community, creative media for pasting, cutting, coloring, and painting for two- and three-dimensional artistic expression, bubble solution in a large tub with different tools for creating bubbles, a climbing wall, and weaving looms. The integrated classroom that we propose clearly makes use of this type of children's museum setting, allowing the child guided choice and a broad array of appropriate activities. The multi-age aspect of such a classroom also supports the possibility of interacting positively with more knowledgeable peers as well as adults.

Gardner proposes the stage from age 7 through about age 14 as appropriate for learning the symbol systems of the culture such as reading, writing, and written mathematical and scientific notation. He does, however, feel that while initially such symbol systems must be taught, they can be mastered basically through working on projects that are interesting and relevant to the child. Projects, then, become the basis for this stage of development. Intrinsic to the use of projects as a means of learning is the *process folio.* Students are encouraged to keep every scrap of planning paper or initial drafts of work (drawings, mappings, scribbles, ideas, etc.) so that, as the project unfolds, student and teacher/mentor can look back on the development for assessment of the thinking and learning process.

Gardner's third stage encompasses age fourteen through young adulthood. In this stage he proposes a "return" to the apprentice/master relationship, with the student having the privilege of working and learning alongside a master in the field. At each stage, his concerns seem to focus on the student having direct experience and application of the concepts and skills required to be a successful learner within a given field. "Real understanding" is critical to Gardner's vision of learning: how the world "interconnects" and integrates knowledge is clearly one of his goals for students (Gardner, 1993).

Gardner is also concerned with the differing learning styles that are part and parcel of multiple intelligences, as well as the "special development trajectory of an individual at promise" (Gardner, 1993, p. 29) within a specific intelligence. He states:

> *Thus, mathematics and music are characterized by the early appearance of gifted children who perform relatively early at or near an adult level. In contrast, the personal intelligences appear to arise much more gradually; prodigies are rare. Moreover, mature performance in one area, does not imply mature performance in another area, just as gifted achievement in one area does not imply gifted achievement in another. (Gardner, 1993, p. 29)*

Each child has a personal way of learning, distinct from anyone else. This personal learning style influences how children approach concept formation and skills development Learning style is not separate from the development of the multiple intelligences. For example, not everyone can learn subtraction by "borrowing," nor reading by using a phonetic approach. Some children may learn subtraction by adding backwards; the thinking involved requires that when subtracting nine from sixteen, one asks "what do I *add* to nine to get to sixteen?" Some children might learn reading through the development of a sight vocabulary. This often entails asking a child what word or words he or she might like to learn today and printing each on a file card for the child to "own." Teachers must know several ways of helping children learn the needed concepts and skills instead of sticking doggedly to whatever method the teacher was taught to use, or has found to be effective for most children in the past.

Components of a Supportive Classroom

If teachers are to provide environments which are responsive to individual differences in learning style and to the development of multiple intelligences, they need to consider all aspects of child development as they plan and interact with the children in their class. The integrated approach, by its nature, supports developmentally appropriate classrooms: multi-age (family) groupings, interactive environments, child-directed projects, and the utilization of music, art, drama, dance, story-telling, and real-world curriculum content. This approach helps to ensure that teachers will, in fact, utilize developmental theory as their guide.

Although each theorist discussed in this chapter focused on a particular aspect of development, it is crucial that the teacher view the child as an integrated whole, taking from each theory but not in an isolated manner.

Piaget informed us that cognitive conflict is necessary to the process of assimilation and accommodation. Curriculum, therefore, must offer novelty but also must be within the child's realm of experiences. If the curriculum is far removed from what the child knows, assimilation cannot take place; if the curriculum offers no challenge, then accommodation cannot take place. The child's own experiences are also germane to Vygotsky's theory: scientific concepts learned in the classroom are dependent on the formation of spontaneous concepts which come from the normal daily activities. The integrated classroom provides many opportunities for children to follow their own interests and engage in activities that have meaning for them. This helps children to develop a belief in themselves as capable of initiating their own learning processes, as well as a sense of mastery and control over the environment that Erikson views as crucial to this stage. Children are intrinsically motivated to discover new information. Because children in the integrated classroom work in multi-age groups, they are exposed to multiple perspectives which challenge their view of the world. Instruction is not designed to teach particular facts nor specific solutions to problems, but is designed to promote the development of thinking skills appropriate for each developmental level and intelligence.

Vygotsky's concept of the zone of proximal development guides the teacher in his or her choice of instructional content for each child. Teaching is not limited to what the child can demonstrate he or she knows, but includes the next level of learning. The integrated approach offers many opportunities for children to work together. Because children are asked to share their experiences in resolving task difficulties, they become aware of their own thinking processes and are more able to direct these processes independently (metacognition and intrapersonal intelligence).

Concrete experiences are the mainstay of the integrated classroom. For the elementary school-age child, direct experience with objects and events is necessary to build complex levels of understanding. A sense of industry versus inferiority requires opportunity for decision making. Choices have to be grounded in the successful accomplishment of tasks. Risk-taking requires a view of self as a problem-solver. In the integrated classroom, teachers are better able to provide activities which can be directly related to the theories of Gardner, Vygotsky, Piaget, and Erikson.

Specific Examples of Application to Classroom Activities Using Attribute Blocks

A direct outcome of "Vygotsky blocks," which were originally designed to assess children's zones of proximal development and their ability to use language as a mediator of thought, are today's "attribute blocks." A typical set of attribute blocks consists of four different shapes (square, circle, triangle, diamond), four different colors (red, blue, yellow, green), and two sizes (large and small).

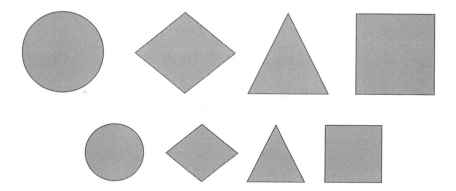

(It is important to note that attribute blocks need teacher guidance and should not be put out for children to use without this guidance.)

Developmental changes in how children think are readily apparent in how they approach working with these blocks. A preoperational child will focus on only one attribute at a time, usually color. An initial activity with these blocks is to have children sort them according to a specific attribute. Watching a child sort the blocks provides insight into the problem-solving strategies being used by the child. This insight can be used for purposes of assessment, planning, and helping the child in the development of metacognitve skills. In another activity, a child is asked to place a block next to a starter block. The second block has to be different in at least one way. Even though the child may choose a block that is different in more than one way, the child at the preoperational stage of development will still focus on only one attribute, be it size, shape, or color, when queried by the teacher. If the teacher asks another child in the group to point out a different attribute, this helps the first child to develop the ability to focus on more than one attribute at a time.

For the child in concrete operations, the teacher may ask the child to choose a block that is different in more than one way and to describe these differences. Attribute blocks are used with small groups of children, providing opportunity for peer interaction, perspective taking, and teacher guidance and mediation. The concrete operational child learns that what is most important and salient to him or her, is not necessarily what is important for others, and that perceptions vary according to individuals.

For the child in formal operations, attribute blocks can be used in challenging and highly interesting ways. Games can be extended to two dimensional, multi-attributes. Students can be asked to form one- and two-difference grids with these blocks, predicting underlying patterns and structure. There are several excellent guides for the use of attribute blocks for ages 5 to 13. One such guide is *Attribute Games and Problems* available from several educational supply companies. An especially good source is *Attribute Games and Activities* by Maria Marolda. This source is also available from educational supply companies.

Gardner stresses the need to teach for thorough understanding; games requiring strategy and reasoning are used extensively in the few schools that are currently following the multiple intelligence theory, such as the Key School in Indianapolis, Indiana, or the New City School in St. Louis, Missouri. Experience with attribute blocks and their varied games can provide not only logical-mathematical understanding, but also ways to improve verbal communication and the ability to "see" differences (linguistic and spatial intelligences). For instance, some children are able to verbally predict just what block might fit into a particular game structure, but have difficulty finding it; while others can instantly pick up the correct block, but cannot accurately verbalize the differences—indications of two completely different strategy approaches. Attribute block games also provide the teacher with practical ways to help children use their game-playing strategies in different subject areas. These game-playing strategies become part of the child's repertoire and can be called upon as needed through metacognitive awareness.

Through attribute block games, children develop social skills. As mentioned previously, perspective taking is an important component of these games. In some of the more complex games, children sometimes need to replace one piece with another in order to complete the grid. Successful negotiation with peers for the necessary replacement requires the development of logical persuasion. Opportunities to be successful with attribute block games are many. Children can achieve academically as well as socially, encouraging competency and the sense of self-worth so important to Erikson's theory.

The successful teacher takes information from developmental theory to assist in the planning and evaluation of curriculum and the assessment of student performance. Classrooms must be constructed so that children have many opportunities for success and an interactive environment responsive to individual differences in learning style and levels of maturity. Children need experiences that contribute to their sense of competency as learners. In addition, the development of social skills and experiences with group life are necessary if a child is not to be handicapped when finding a place for him- or herself in the society of his or her peers. The philosophy behind the integrated classroom supports a healthy, developmentally appropriate environment, with a teacher who clearly understands how children in a particular stage of development think and relate to their world, and how they change over time.

Suggested Activities

These activities will assist you in integrating the developmental theories addressed in this chapter. Observing children and recording their behavior helps to make theories "real." These activities also will provide you with opportunities to see how a knowledge of developmental theories can be helpful in creating an appropriate learning environment for children.

Observe three different children in the same classroom who are approximately the same age. Compare and contrast their developmental levels. Do the same observation with three children who are of markedly different ages; a 6-year-old, a 9-year-old, and an 11-year-old.

Pick two children and look for indicators of which intelligences are their strengths, and how, or if, the classroom is supporting these strengths.

Identify these children's weaker intelligences, and consider how these intelligences can be strengthened within the classroom environment.

Try a series of Piagetian conservation tasks with children of different ages. Record their answers before and after the transformation. Determine if the child is preoperational or in concrete or formal operations.

Observe a child with an older peer or adult in a supermarket, shopping mall, or restaurant. Note how the older peer or adult mediates the environment for the child and how this mediation might be culture specific.

Suggested Readings

In addition to the references listed at the end of this chapter, the following readings are suggested to help broaden your understanding of developmental theory and how theory relates to practice. We recommend that you consider purchasing a recently published child development text to provide a basis for understanding development over the life cycle.

Clay, Marie M. (1991). *Becoming Literate. The Construction of Inner Control*. New Hampshire: Heinemann Educational Books, Inc.

DeVries, Rheta and Kohlberg, Lawrence. (1987). *Constructivist Early Education: Overview and Comparison With Other Programs*. Washington, D.C.: National Association for the Education of Young Children

Erikson, Erik H. (1963). *Childhood and Society*. Toronto: George J. McLeod Ltd.

Erikson, Erik H. (1968). *Identity, Youth and Crisis*. New York: W.W. Norton and Company.

Furth, Hans G. (1970). *Piaget for Teachers*. New Jersey: Prentice-Hall Inc.

Garvey, Catherine. (1984). *Children's Talk*. Massachusetts: Harvard University Press.

Gilligan, Carol. (1982). *In a Different Voice: Psychological Theory in Women's Development*. Massachusetts: Harvard University Press.

Ginsberg, Herbert and Opper, Sylvia (1979). *Piaget's Theory of Intellectual Development*. New Jersey: Prentice-Hall, Inc.

Glasser, William. (1984). *Control Theory*. New York: Harper and Row Publishers.

Hawkins, Frances Pockman. (1974). *The Logic of Action*. New York: Pantheon Books.

Hendrick, Joanne. (1984). *The Whole Child*. Missouri: Times, Mirror-Mosby

Kamii, Constance K. (1985). *Young Children Reinvent Arithmetic: Implications of Piaget's Theory*. New York: Teachers College Press.

Kamii, Constance K. (1989). *Young Children Continue to Reinvent Arithmetic*. New York: Teachers College Press.

Kamii, Constance and DeVries, Rheta. (1980). *Group Games in Early Education: Implications of Piaget's Theory*. Washington D.C.: National Association for Supervision and Curriculum Development.

Piaget, Jean. (1968). *Six Psychological Studies*. New York: Vintage Books

Samples, Bob, Charles, Cheryl, and Barnhart, Dick. (1977). *The Wholeschool Book*. Massachusetts: Addison-Wesley Publishing Company.

Stoessiger, Rex and Edmunds, Joy. (1992). *Natural Learning in Mathematics*. New Hampshire: Heinemann Educational Books.

Wadsworth, Barry J. (1984). *Piaget's Theory of Cognitive and Affective Development*. New York: Longman Inc.

Whitin, David J., Mills, Heidi, O'Keefe, Timothy. (1990). *Living and Learning Mathematics*. New Hampshire: Heinemann Educational Books.

Vygotsky, Lev. (1962). *Thought and Language*. Massachusetts: MIT Press.

References

Berk, Laura E. (1991). *Child Development*. Boston: Allyn Bacon.
Cole, Michael, John-Steiner, Vera, Scribner, Sylvia, Souberman, Ellen, eds. (1978). *Mind in Society*. Massachusetts: Harvard University Press.
Collis, Mark and Dalton, Joan. (1990). *Becoming Responsible Learners*. New Hampshire: Heinemann Press.
Crain, William. (1992). *Theories of Development*. New Jersey: Prentice-Hall, Inc.
Erikson, Erik. (1982). *The Life Cycle Completed*. New York: W.W. Norton.
Gardner, Howard. (1985). *Frames of Mind*. New York: Basic Books.
Gardner, Howard. (1991). *The Unschooled Mind*. New York: Basic Books.
Gardner, Howard. (1993). *Multiple Intelligences: The Theory in Practice*. New York: Basic Books.
Labinowicz, ed. (1980). *The Piaget Primer*. California: Addison-Wesley Publishing Company, Inc.

Overton, Willis F. (1972). *A New Look at Progressive Education.* Virginia: Association for Supervision and Curriculum Development.

Piaget, Jean and Inhelder, Barbel. (1969). *The Psychology of the Child.* New York: Basic Books.

Seifert, Kevin L. and Hoffnung, Robert J. (1991). *Child and Adolescent Development* Boston: Houghton Mifflin Company.

Thomas, Mary R. (1992). *Comparing Theories of Child Development.* California: Wadsworth Publishing.

Tribe, Carol. (1982). *Profile of Three Theories.* Iowa: Kendall-Hunt.

3

The Learning Environment

For many years the school architect was considered the creator of the learning envi-ronment while the teacher was seen as housekeeper, arranging, provisioning, and decorating. Teachers considered the learning environment as a kind of scenery for teaching and learning, a pleasant yet inert background for classroom life.

However, there is another way of looking at the learning environment and the teacher's role in creating it within an architectural facility. This view recog-nizes the teacher-arranged environment as an active and pervasive influence on the lives of children and teachers throughout the school day. In the processes of teaching and learning, the physical environment arranged by the teacher has two functions. It provides the setting for learning and at the same time acts as a participant in teaching and learning. (Loughlin and Suina, 1982, p. 1)

The physical environment reflects the teacher's ideas about how children learn, their relationship to one another, and his or her own role. In class-rooms in which the teacher perceives his or her role as central to all class-room activity, one would expect to see an environment in which communi-cation is primarily directed to and comes from the teacher. Materials and equipment in such a classroom are under teacher control, with the teacher determining when children should have access to these materials and equip-ment and monitoring their use closely. The teacher who perceives his or her role more as a facilitator would be more apt to have a classroom environment which encourages communication between children, and where materials and equipment are distributed around the classroom so that children can use them according to what activities or projects they are pursuing.

It is not possible to understand children's behavior or the outcomes of curriculum without considering the effect of the physical space. The physical environment "pulls" children to certain activities and behaviors, and not to others. It is almost as though the physical environment has a "voice" that children hear above the voice of the adult in the classroom. A large open space tells children to run and tumble. Shelves that are disorganized, where it difficult to know where to replace an item, or where materials are not clearly displayed and marked, invite children to take materials haphazardly and to return them in a careless fashion. The classrooms described in "Windows" are two contrasting examples, again extreme, that demonstrate the strength of environmental effects.

A Window into Two Classrooms

Classroom 1: A Traditional Fifth Grade

Children are arranged in ten-desk clusters, facing each other. There are two such clusters parallel to each other in this classroom with the remaining eight across the back of the room, leaving a large empty space in the middle. The teacher's desk occupies a prominent position at the front and side of the room (see Figure 3-1).

The children are beginning a unit on colonial America and have just finished watching a video describing the architecture and furnishings of homes typical of New England, the midwest and southern states. The teacher follows up the video with a question session to assess the children's learning of pertinent facts and critical concepts. Satisfied with the answers received from the children, the teacher proceeds to assign the reading (from the history text) and the writing (from the accompanying workbook). Additional resources available to the children are a set of encyclopedias and a half-dozen books checked out of the school library. Other materials, such as paper (construction, final product writing "stationery," and good white illustration paper), crayons, markers, pencils, and rulers are all neatly arranged in cupboards awaiting the teacher's direction to a child to pass out these supplies or the teacher passing them out him- or herself. The teacher has carefully given the assignment and asks if there are any questions before setting the students to work.

The children slowly begin to rummage in their desks for the textbook and workbook, pencils, and whatever else they feel they might need. Having been "released" from paying attention to the video and the teacher's directions, they begin to converse with each other not only about the assigned work, but also about borrowing needed materials from friends, and about other social and nonacademic events in their lives. After about ten minutes of such behavior, the teacher begins to issue warnings: "You need to settle down now." "You should be getting at your assignments." "I want it quiet in here, some people are trying to work." "I like the way Jesse and Johnnie are working quietly at their desks." "Those children who have

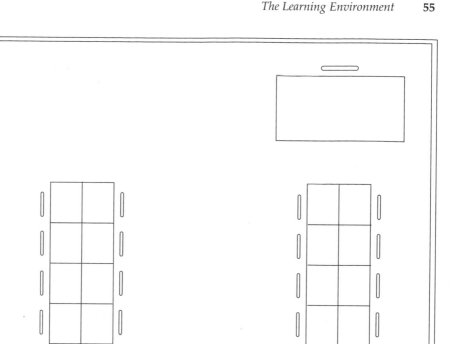

FIGURE 3-1   Window into Two Classrooms—Traditional Fifth Grade

not finished answering the questions at the end of the chapter will have to forfeit recess to finish—you have ample time to complete this assignment!"

Several times during this "seat work assignment," children come to ask the teacher for supplies that are housed in the cupboards. Sometimes the teacher gets the wanted material, other times he or she directs the child to the cupboard. Getting these supplies takes time and draws attention away from the task for both children and teacher. Upon returning to their seats, some children find it difficult to get back on task. When children need to cross the room to talk with the teacher or get supplies, they often get "trapped" in the dead space in the middle of the room, which results in some minor but annoying playing around. There are many admonishments by the teacher for the children to "get to work."

Classroom 2: An Integrated, Multi-Age Third, Fourth, and Fifth Grade

The children in this classroom are also studying colonial America and have just finished watching the same video on architecture and interior furnishings. They are now seated on the floor in their meeting area, brainstorming with the teacher all of the possible topics that could be researched pertaining to the main theme. After the brainstorming session, the children make a list of questions that they wish to pursue. The teacher then asks them to decide which topics and questions they want to tackle first, and to sign their names in the appropriate place on the large chart they have just completed. The children then disperse in pairs or small groups to begin their research.

Children space themselves all over the room in the workspaces provided. Each workspace is provisioned with pencils, markers, crayons, papers of several varieties, rulers, compasses, construction materials such as clay, popsicle sticks, cardboard boxes, matte board, glues, and scissors. Materials are both easily accessible and plentiful. Workspaces clearly limit the number of children who can be accommodated by the number of chairs placed at the tables or by a sign that states "three children may work here." Books are everywhere, in each workspace as well as in the "reading corner." Selections include encyclopedias, dictionaries, textbooks, fiction, biography, books on architectural design, and blueprints of colonial style houses.

Most children immediately settle into their initial research, planning and organizing how they will present their work to the rest of the class. Because the greater number of children are working independently, the teacher is better able to direct those children who need additional help in getting started. If a child needs some material that is not in his or her workspace, or needs information from another source, pathways in this classroom are carefully planned and constructed so that others are not disturbed by movement (see Figure 3-2).

Importance of the Learning Environment

As demonstrated in "Windows," crucial to a smoothly operating integrated classroom is the environment, from the physical arrangement of furniture and storage units to the provisioning of workspaces. As noted previously, the learning environment sends out powerful messages to children, so powerful that these messages frequently override any verbal directions given by the teacher. How and where workspaces are constructed will even determine whether they get used, how frequently, and in what way.

An example of just how powerful the physical environment can be, even for adults who have been carefully instructed in procedures, follows.

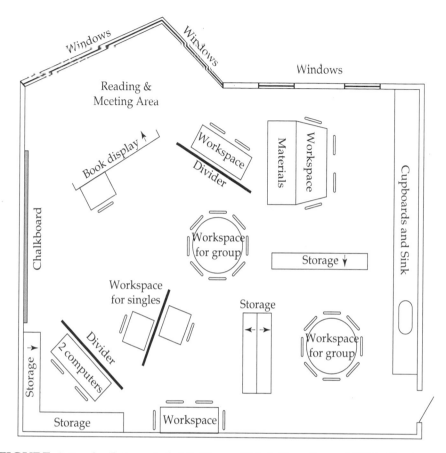

FIGURE 3-2   An Integrated, Multi-age Third, Fourth, and Fifth Grade

During a summer workshop for teachers, a major problem arose. The entire workshop occupied one wing of a school.

The teacher participants had been told on the first day to check the bulletin boards each morning to find what was being offered that day and when; they were then to sign up for their desired class session and get themselves to the designated meeting area without being called. What in fact happened was that the teacher participants entered through the workroom (see Figure 3-3) for coffee, then proceeded into the section of the main area where tables were set up for playing games outside the workroom. Teachers never got out of this space—at least not without a great deal of prodding from the workshop staff! The workshop staff found themselves asking each participant if he or she had indeed read the bulletin board, signed up for what they wanted to attend, and knew when and where his or her chosen

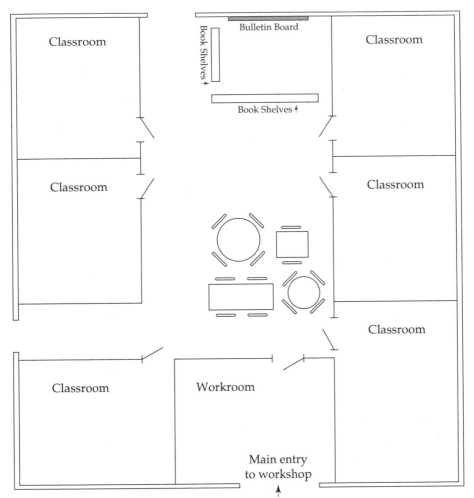

FIGURE 3-3   Teacher's Summer Workshop—Original Physical Environment

session was meeting. This problem persisted well into the second week of the six-week workshop. Workshop staff found themselves getting very upset and angry at participants for taking so little responsibility for themselves and their learning, even to the point that some uncharitable remarks about their suitability as teachers were creeping into staff meetings. "Perhaps teaching is not their forte—catering maybe!" "If the children in their classrooms acted like this, they would have a fit!"

A visit from an expert in classroom environment neatly solved the problem. By brainstorming with the teachers and workshop staff, the decision was made to rearrange the main meeting are, as shown in Figure 3-4).

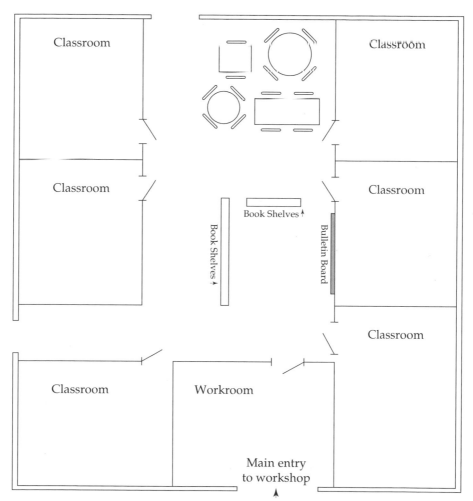

FIGURE 3-3   Teacher's Summer Workshop—Redesigned

Miracle of miracles—it really worked! The balance of the workshop days rolled along smoothly, with the teacher participants arriving, still getting their coffee on the way in, but proceeding directly into the area where the daily messages, schedules, and sign-up sheets were posted. Morning talk between participants centered around what was going on that day, when and where, instead of just the "trivia" of previous exchanges. Everyone's attitude, including that of the workshop staff, improved, and the business of learning proceeded in a powerful way. The workshop staff had learned a painful but forceful lesson about the impact of the environment and jokingly referred to their previous error of placing the tables and chairs in such a socially inviting way as "the sidewalk cafe." Indeed, the environment can be a powerful instructional assistant, or it can work against its daily inhabitants.

Teachers often have the same problem in setting up their classrooms as did these workshop leaders, with the actual result differing from the intended result. For example, the popular desk arrangement found in the traditional classroom in "Windows 1," may be planned to encourage interaction between children around academic tasks; however, the result is often off-task behavior in the form of socializing because of the number of children in the space and the visual impact of the "banquet table" arrangement. This arrangement invites a great deal of verbal interchange, whether it's to ask someone at the other end of the row for a supply or about last night's television show. Children at one end of this formation are just as apt to "yell down" to the other end as to talk quietly with their immediate neighbor. Teachers who use this kind of classroom arrangement frequently spend a great portion of their day asking for quiet and urging children to get to work. Teachers must plan the environment in the same way they plan all aspects of curriculum. The environment and the curriculum are interdependent.

Three Components of the Environment

There are three major components to the environment which need to be carefully considered: the architectural environment, the arranged environment (Loughlin and Suina, 1982), and the provisioned environment. The architectural environment is what is there; it is the way a room is constructed. This includes the shape and size of the rooms, the number and placement of windows, electrical outlets, heating units, sink, and permanently built-in storage space. The arranged environment is what furnishings are used and where they are placed into inviting and smoothly functioning workspaces. These furnishings include tables of different sizes, shapes, and heights, chairs, stools, benches, movable shelving, storage areas such as cubbies and bins, and soft areas with comfortable seating such as bean bag chairs and cushions, and carpet. The provisioned environment is the materials and resources that go into a workspace; the work cards and guided explorations and the appropriate accompanying materials (for example, blocks, scales, weights, and measures), as well as the raw materials (for example, papers, pencils, fibers, paints, junk box materials, glues, and pastes).

The Architectural Space

The architectural environment cannot be changed. Surprisingly, not all classrooms are rectangular. Figures 3-5 and 3-6 show some examples of real physical spaces from real schools.

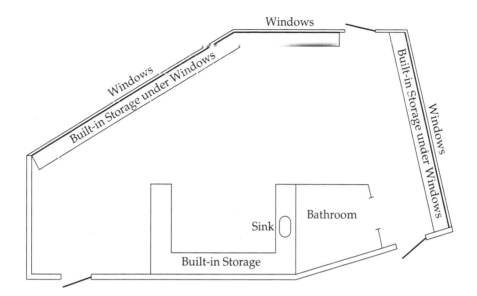

FIGURE 3-5 An Unusually Shaped Classroom

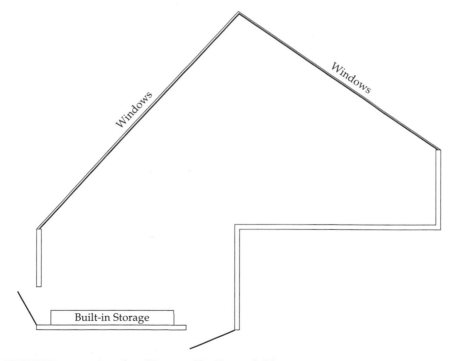

FIGURE 3-6 Another Unusually Shaped Classroom

Optimal use of the existing space requires careful decision making. For example, south-facing windows will generate more heat for the room and will make a better area for greenhouse growth experiments than ones facing north, west, or east.

The space for chalkboards and bulletin boards might be limited because of the number of windows or cabinets in the room. Moving these items may be impossible, but lowering them to accommodate young children's height may be easily arranged. Shelving and cupboards that are built into spaces too high for children to reach must be kept for excess materials or for materials that will be rotated into workspaces throughout the year. The architectural space invites certain activities and discourages others, dictating to a certain degree how the room can be arranged.

We recommend making a scale drawing of the classroom. Use 18" by 24" graph paper with four squares to the inch. The scale should be one-half inch on the drawing to one foot in the classroom. Mark windows, doors, permanent shelving, cupboard space, carpeted and uncarpeted areas of the floor, location of sink and electrical outlets, as well as unusual spaces such as bay windows and odd-angle corners. This drawing will assist the teacher throughout the year in making decisions about room arrangement and in mapping traffic patterns.

The Arranged Environment

Once the architectural environment is clearly understood, the next step is to plan for the arranged environment. With the use of drawings of commonly used classroom furniture on the appropriate scale of one half inch to one foot along with a drawing of the classroom space, workspaces can be designed. Consideration must be given to the number of workspaces that will be needed to accommodate the number of children in the room, as well as to the kinds of furnishings that will meet the needs of children as they interact and work on projects in all academic areas. For example, if there are twenty-four children in the group, there must be twenty-four spaces provided for work of various kinds. The need for twenty-four spaces does not mean that there must be twenty-four chairs at or around tables. Spaces can be varied in size, shape, and content, with furnishings to provide for multiple ways for children to spend their day: working as a whole class, in small groups of three to four, in pairs, or individually depending on the activities and the immediate needs of the children. An area designed for the entire class to meet as a group can be on the carpeted floor. This space should be just large enough to accommodate the whole group without children sitting on top of each other, and without having so much room as to invite running, playing room tag, wrestling, or like behaviors. This large space works better in a corner or on a side of the room, rather than in the center. The center location tends to become "dead space."

> *When children are drawn into dead space, they tend to stay in it, because there aren't clear paths to lead them out. Since the space is empty of materials to influence or focus activity, dead space tends to generate a boisterous, loose socialization or disorganized physical movement. In older children, this takes the form of teasing, roughhousing, mock fighting, or some flirting; younger children resort to disorganized running, chasing, roughhousing and sliding. (Loughlin and Suina, 1982, pp. 65, 66)*

Furniture should be varied. Tables must be of different heights depending on the activity taking place in that space. Children can work efficiently on the floor, on chairs, on stools, or standing. The shapes and sizes of tables influence the amount and kind of social interaction, as well as how children approach and sustain the academic activity. A round table which seats six children comfortably works beautifully for a teacher-directed session. A small rectangular table pushed against a divider with two chairs side-by-side may invite a cooperative learning effort. If the same two chairs are placed across from each other, children tend to spend more time socializing.

The determination of areas for activities should take into consideration noise level and the need for physical movement. For example, a comfortable reading area should be in a part of the room that is quiet and away from spaces where children are physically interacting with materials. A reading area should have good light. A part of the room adjacent to the windows affording natural light is a good choice. The reading area also requires adequate storage for books and magazines, as well as electrical outlets for headphones and tape recorders which permit children to read along or listen to stories.

Technology of all kinds must play a very central role in classrooms for the twenty-first century. However, computers, video disc players, VCRs, and CD ROMs can be "attractive nuisances" in the classroom, drawing children other than those currently working with them into a spectator status. It is therefore important to think about proper placement of these technological resources. Creating spaces away from the central traffic patterns is crucial. Computer and video monitor screens should be facing *into* a corner space and *not* into the classroom so that passersby are not drawn into the area by an intriguing picture. Where radiation is a factor, dividers or storage units can be placed to cover the back of the equipment. Multiple outlets should be nearby in order to prevent children from tripping over wires or overloading the circuits. All of this equipment should be on rolling tables so that whole-class use is possible.

In addition to spaces for whole-group activities, reading, and technology, there must be spaces provided for quiet observation of nature and the physical world as well as other science-oriented explorations, use of mathematics manipulatives, drawing and painting, writing, and construction. Most classrooms are not architecturally constructed to accommodate all these spaces easily. Dividers and movable storage units allow for creative space-making, and also permit changes throughout the year as the children's interests and activities change. If children are not using a particular space, it is important to determine why. It may be because what is there cannot be easily seen, and therefore does not draw children into the area. A child's eye level is very different from that of an adult. It is important to view the room from a child's perspective. The teacher, after setting up his or her room, should get down to the height of the smallest child in the class in order to gain this perspective. Being pushed around the room on a low stool with wheels while videotaping can enhance an understanding of the child's view. This kind of planning and organizing does take time, but the outcome can be children who are actively engaged, thus requiring less teacher direction, particularly around behavioral expectations.

Movable storage units provide excellent display spaces for children's work: the backs of bookcases, room dividers made either of wood or particle board, and even the back of an upright piano can be turned into attractive and useful display space by covering the area on which work is to be displayed with suitable backing material. Again, if the displays are to be utilized by children as part of the learning environment, they have to be at children's eye level. If children are expected to create these display areas, they must be within the children's reach. Teachers need sufficient numbers of bulletin boards of different sizes in different areas of the room. Bulletin boards are necessary so that lists of specific lessons and groupings of children, lunch decisions, attendance, and messages about special events can be posted. Children should be encouraged to utilize these communications not only for experience in reading but also to avoid taking time away from the day's activities. For example, a teacher of 5-, 6- and 7-year-olds plans for an interesting special activity daily, such as going to the garden at ten o'clock to weed and water. The bulletin board posting of this event requires children to sign below the notice if they want to be included in this group. If the teacher leaves six spaces for signatures, this indicates that only six people may take part in this event that day.

Every child, as well as the teacher, should have a personal space in the classroom. Standard cubbies or those created by milk crates or empty boxes work better than individual desks for the storage of personal items. Storage spaces in desks are difficult to organize and act as a distracter for on-task behavior. In the integrated classroom, most spaces and materials are shared since cooperative endeavors are a major component of instruction. A place where children can keep a treasured item or clothing helps promote a sense of well-being and security. Teachers, too, need space that is their own. However, a large desk takes up unnecessary space. Shelving which is too high for children to reach or a separate closet can serve as the teacher's space. In addition, the teacher needs a space for small group lessons. Children know when they come to this space that the teacher will direct the activity, and that this space is usually not available for children's projects.

To set up an environment that truly meets the needs of children and the teacher's instructional goals does not require a small fortune, but still may be difficult even for the most supportive school district to fund. This means, for the committed teacher, the need to SCROUNGE and TRADE! If a colleague has a table that isn't being used and the teacher of the integrated classroom has too many chairs, maybe a trade can be effected. Trades like this are possible around size and shape of tables, heights of chairs, room dividers, and movable storage. Garage and rummage sales are excellent sources of discarded furniture which, with a little paint, make excellent workspaces. The classroom may not, on day one, look exactly the way the teacher envisions, but with thought, ingenuity, and planning, furniture and materials can be acquired over time. Children's input into the setting up of the classroom environment can assist the teacher in creatively utilizing limited resources. Helping the teacher design the classroom gives ownership to the children. This sense of ownership encourages children to maintain the environment and utilize it in constructive ways.

The Provisioned Environment

Most standard classrooms are virtually barren of raw materials, of things, and are overloaded with prepared materials, heavily scored with predetermined routes which allow only bogus exploration. The raw materials component of the environment is extremely important. The human components must make possible uses of the materials in accordance with the child's intent and perception of the inherent properties of the materials. By raw materials I mean all kinds of things, from pencils and paper to books and string and magnets and bottles and boxes and paint and clay and mirrors and animals and . . . (Anthony Kallet, in Yeomans, 1969, p. 13)

The most appropriate furnishings, perfectly arranged, will not sustain the interest or promote the growth and development of important concepts and skills, if what is offered to the children for work and exploration over the length of the school day is not challenging, interesting, and developmentally appropriate. Not only *what* is provisioned but *how* it is contained and presented will directly influence what occurs.

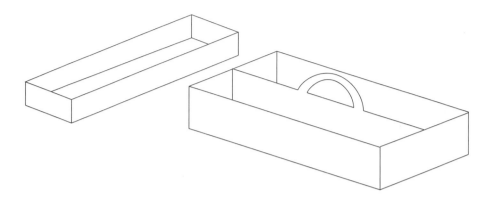

Each workspace, whether its contents directly relate to reading and writing skills or not, must be provisioned with materials that will encourage writing or some visual representation of what children are doing. Materials should include pens, pencils, thick and thin colored markers, crayons, rulers, scissors, glue, and clear and masking tape. These items can be neatly arranged in a plastic work basket or a low-sided box.

If recording materials are not easily accessible within the workspace, it is almost a certainty that writing/recording will not occur. When children have to interrupt their work by leaving a workspace, their train of thought as well as their concentration is broken. Children on a quest for materials are often drawn to what others are doing elsewhere in the room, and it is difficult for them to get back to their own projects. Even areas where writing material usually is not found should have them. For example, markers, pencils, different sizes of papers, and tape for posting in a block area can encourage children to label items and write signs. For beginners in literacy acquisition, this kind of activity is most important.

Raw Materials

Raw materials are a critical component of an integrated classroom; blocks appropriate to different ages and activities, paints, crayons, chalk, clay, fabric, yarn and string, measuring cups and spoons, collections of containers of different sizes and shapes, construction materials, plastic bottles, and paper towel tubes become useful items for student projects. Milk cartons of varying sizes can be used for measuring liquids and are easily replaced as they wear out. Paper towel tubes can be used in construction as well as for experimentation with bubbles and bubble solutions. Raw materials basically can be experimented with, shaped, reshaped, and manipulated in multiple ways. With the exception of building blocks, which are a permanent fixture, most raw materials will need replacing from time to time. Publishing houses, including newspapers, are great sources for different sizes, colors, and textures of paper and are very willing to give their scraps to classrooms. Frame shops are great sources for scrap matte board, either for free or at minimal cost.

Tools

Tools provide a variety of functions. They allow the child to process materials or information. They can serve specific needs, such as calculating, measuring, recording, joining, cutting, shaping, mixing, viewing, communicating, and heating and cooling (Loughlin and Suina, 1982). Computing tools include such things as Cuisenaire rods, geoboards, chip trading materials, abaci, calculators, computers and their requisite programs for all levels of children, plus the addition of discrete materials such as large buttons, keys, inch, half-inch, or centimeter cubes, toy cars, toy animals, and unifix cubes for counting. One also can add attribute blocks and pattern blocks for sorting and classifying. Helpful measuring tools include all kinds of rulers— unmarked straight-edges, yard sticks, meter sticks, tape measures, and trundle wheels—as well as stop watches and measuring cups and spoons. What is important is to have a variety of these measuring tools available to enable the child to choose the tool most helpful to him or her for a specific task.

Recording, expressing, and communicating tools need some special attention. Included in this category are tape recorders, still cameras and video cameras, as well as the more commonly thought of pencils, markers, crayons, paints, and chalks. For children who cannot yet write their ideas and thoughts easily, a tape recorder makes the task very possible. It is important for children to understand that there are many different ways of recording one's own work—drawing, painting, charting, graphing, tape-recording, photographing, or videotaping—and that one way is not necessarily better than another. Children's choices of how best to record their work often reflects a strength in one of the multiple intelligences, and permitting or encouraging such variety builds in chances to gain competency in lots of ways.

Information Sources

Information sources can take on many forms. The classroom should be provisioned with lots of books at different reading levels, covering all possible subject areas from great works of art to cookbooks. Information sources can be extended to include posters, pamphlets, picture files, slides, video tapes and discs, records, and audio tapes, each of which stores information in a different way. Live animals in the classroom provide information and encourage sensitive and accurate observational skills. Further information sources are telephone books, catalogs, atlases, maps, blueprints, word lists built around specific topics or concepts, as well as the more conventional reference materials such as dictionaries of different types and levels, encyclopedias, almanacs, newspapers, and magazines. The more information sources relate to the real world, the better. For example, children are fascinated by using materials usually found only in mom or dad's office or at home. The providing of a variety of information sources underscores for the children the huge amount of resources available for problem solving and project development

Containers

Containers are used for a variety of purposes. They hold materials for specific projects suggested in workspaces, and also suggest to children how the materials should be used. These containers can range from brightly spray-painted "flats" (cut-down boxes from cases of soft drinks) to round, five-gallon ice cream cylinders, milk cartons of varying sizes, buckets, bowls, pans, yogurt containers, shoe boxes, toolkits, and even envelopes. There is a need for watertight containers for explorations with liquids, as well as for mixing, using, and storing paints. Trays make excellent containers for holding materials that belong together. Styrofoam meat trays from the supermarket are useful holders for markers, crayons, pencils, and pens. Shape, storage capacity, size, and adaptability of containers are important factors to consider. Materials must be contained in storage boxes that enhance the use of the material as well as invite easy return of the material for storage and future use. If a child cannot find a material, the materials will not be used. Just putting a label on a closed box, no matter how large or brightly colored, will not attract a child to its contents. Having materials or games in open flat boxes immediately impacts the visual sense and lets the child know what is available. Containers covered with bold prints, plaids, or multicolored contact paper often distract children from what is *in* the box and adds unnecessary visual stimulation to the classroom. Empty containers also should be available for children to store their projects in process. Having a container to hold all parts of a project in process is a major contributor to encouraging extended and thoughtful work.

Large boxes with dividers labeled with each child's name and placed in a central location for ease of use help children file work that needs completing, and also provides teachers (and parents) with ongoing information for assessment.

Well-arranged classrooms with thoughtfully provisioned work areas will sustain children's interest and help to maintain appropriate behavior. This environment will act as an "instructional assistant" to the teacher so that he or she can work with small groups or individuals without major interruptions.

The physical environment speaks more directly to children in terms of behavioral and academic expectations than do posted rules or spoken directions. The physical environment supports independent activity on the part of children, increasing their ability to self-direct their learning and become responsible for themselves and their surroundings. When children are responsibly and actively engaged with their own projects, research, and learning, the teacher is better able to watch and assess, guide, lead, coach, ask pertinent questions, and encourage academic risk-taking, as well as teach directly when necessary. The following quote from an upper elementary grade teacher sums up the interaction between teacher, child, and the environment most accurately:

> *I believe very strongly that children must ultimately take responsibility for their own learning. They can be trusted to make decisions that are best for themselves, both socially and academically. Therefore it is my job to provide information, materials, opportunities, and guidance for every child, and help them make those important learning decisions. I cannot make someone learn; I can, and do, motivate, encourage, and create a safe environment where risks are easily taken. (Letter to parents by Jan Bradford, 1993)*

Suggested Activities: Analyzing the Environment

1. Make an "aerial view" sketch on $8\frac{1}{2}$" by 11" paper of the existing classroom, indicating windows, doors, and permanently installed shelves, cupboards, sinks, etc. Draw in the desk/table arrangement. Make about a dozen photocopies.

2. Using one of your classroom maps, watch the traffic patterns used by the children for about fifteen to twenty minutes. Pick a time when children have the option to select activities. Each time a child gets up and moves, indicate this on the drawing, showing where the child goes, whether he or she stops along the way, and the return route. After the time is up, look at the drawing and think about the following questions: Do children interrupt each other as they pass by? Do they go find what they want immediately or do they need to hunt or ask? Are there parts of the room that are seemingly never used? Do children tend to congregate in one area? Are there specific areas that are overcrowded or overused?

3. Using one of your classroom maps, choose one child to observe over a time period of fifteen to twenty minutes. Indicate where the child is when the observation begins, and show where the child goes every time he or she moves. Also note if the child stops to interact with a peer, how long this takes, and when the child returns to whatever quest was begun. After the time is up, analyze the "mapping" and think about the following questions: Was the child's attention on the task or project at hand? How long was the child actually on-task? Were the materials needed for the task in the workspace, or did the child have to search or request? Did the child interrupt others in his or her search for what he or she needed? Did the child easily get back on-task after getting what he or she wanted?

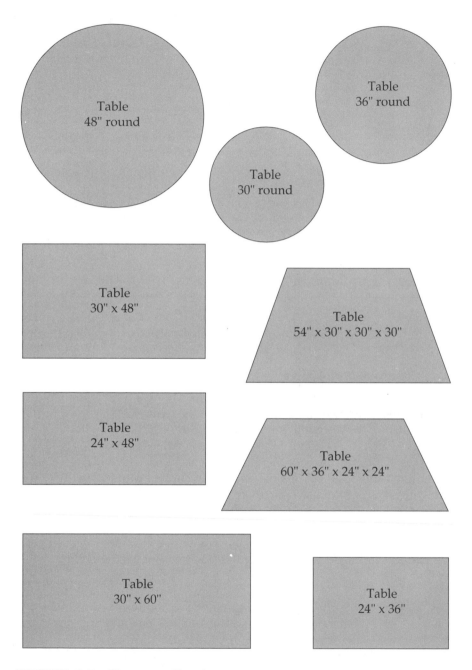

FIGURE 3-7   Classroom Furniture

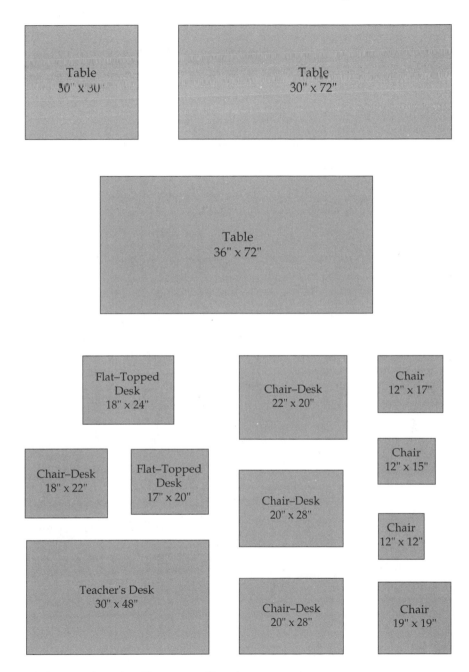

FIGURE 3-7(cont)   Classroom Furniture

4. Pick an area or workspace to observe for fifteen to twenty minutes. Using one of your classroom maps, indicate the following: What materials are there? What materials are being used? Are they returned to their proper containers and spaces after use? What materials never seem to be chosen? Why do you think this is happening? Is the material chosen used in that workspace or carried off to another? If you want a particular material used more frequently, how might this be accomplished?

5. Make a scale drawing of the classroom, using the scale of one-half inch to one foot. Use a large sheet of graph paper with four squares to the inch. Mark all windows, doors, permanently installed cupboards, shelf space, sinks, etc. Indicate carpeted and tiled areas. Photocopy Figure 3-7 and use this furniture to rearrange the room so that traffic is dispersed more evenly. Create workspaces for pairs, small group, and large group experiences. (If there is furniture in the classroom that is not in Figure 3-7, draw your own pieces, using the one-half inch to one foot scale.) Try arrangements that are truly different, such as nothing at right angles and arranging from the "middle out" rather than from the "walls in." Be sure to include chairs in each arrangement, because they make a huge difference in walking space! Think about creating workspaces for the number of children in the class, but not necessarily desk/chair or table/chair space. Create spaces for individuals, pairs, small group, and large group experiences. Consider the light for each space, both natural and artificial. Think about what will be noisy and quiet areas. Give one of your arrangements a real try with the children. Reevaluate and try again! Ask the children for suggestions!

References

Loughlin, Catherine and Suina, Joseph. (1982). *The Learning Environment: An Instructional Strategy.* New York: Teachers College Press.

Yeomans, Edward. (1969). *Education for Initiative and Responsibility.* Massachusetts: National Association of Independent Schools.

4

Developing the Responsible Learner

When the child's need to be competent is satisfied, motivation for further achievement is enhanced: deprived of opportunities for success, young people express their frustration through troubled behavior or by retreating in helplessness and inferiority. (Brendtro et al., 1990, p. 39)

In every classroom, there are many opportunities for children to develop perceptions of themselves as competent and responsible learners. Children can be encouraged to take risks, become independent problem solvers, and learn to engage in socially responsible behavior. Children also can have experience after experience in which they are compared to more "capable" peers or siblings and given little opportunity to direct their own learning or to work cooperatively on tasks with peers. The responsible learner is an independent learner, one who trusts him- or herself to construct knowledge in meaningful ways and who perceives failure as a step in the process to success.

A Window into Two Classrooms

Classroom 1: A Traditional Second Grade

The teacher has decided that it would be fun for her children to make bunny pictures as part of their science lesson on baby animals that are usually born in the spring. Children are making these spring bunnies to be displayed on their classroom windows. Each child has been given a teacher-made picture of a bunny to cut and decorate. Children are sitting at tables of six. On each table are scissors, crayons, paste, and cotton balls. The teacher has made a sample bunny for children to copy. A number of the children are complaining that they did this project last year in their first grade classroom. The teacher is constantly called to assist a child who claims he does not know how to make the bunny look like the teacher's. One child is becoming very frustrated because she cannot make the scissors work. Another child asks the teacher if he can use buttons for the bunny's eyes. The teacher replies that buttons are not part of this project.

Classroom 2: An Integrated Primary Classroom of Children 5, 6, and 7 Years Old

Children are busily decorating their room to support a project on the season changing from winter to spring. Children are spread all over the room, working at tables and on the floor. There is an array of materials available in each workspace to suggest different aspects of plant and animal growth. Materials include basic art supplies as well as junk material, construction material, books and picture files that depict seasonal changes, along with writing paper and pencils. There are no adult-made models of decorations for children to copy, nor are there a set of directions that children are expected to follow in the creation of these decorations. Their work is directly tied to a project that has been pursued over the past few weeks, giving children many ideas about change and growth. Children are working in small groups, alone, or in pairs, depending upon what they have decided to do. One child has difficulty using a scissors. Another child lends assistance as a normal act of cooperation. The children decide where to post the output of their morning's work; their discussion revolves around how to group and organize the plants and animals they have made.

The Responsible Learner Defined

It would be expected that a child who was responsible for his or her own learning would have certain attributes that would set him or her apart from his or her classmates. For one, the child would be self-directed, not requiring many external motivators in the form of rewards. He or she would be a child willing to take risks, and would demonstrate this by an eagerness to try new things that extend beyond the safe and comfortable. This child could be trusted to make choices about how to spend time in the classroom. The teacher, in working with such a child, would provide opportunities for independent and cooperative activity and the child would use this time wisely. The child expects to succeed, and does so.

There are many children in classrooms who have the potential to be like the one described above. The integrated classroom supports responsible behavior on the part of the child, and discourages teachers from the use of external control and power which can interfere with the development of self-responsible behavior.

The Relationship of the Responsible Learner to the Integrated Classroom

The integrated classroom supports curriculum as an outcome of children's interests within the parameters of teacher and community expectations for educational goals. A child, able to pursue his or her own interests is likely to do so without a great deal of teacher intervention. For the responsible learner, the process of learning becomes as important as the product or outcome of learning. For example, a child interested in the area of space travel has pertinent questions about this topic that she would like to pursue. These questions guide research, the finding of resources, and the exploration of these resources. The answers to her questions often lead to more questions which continues the process of exploration and research. Within this research process, because of the maximum time permitted for practice, the mastery of reading, writing, and organizational skills are promoted. This process also gives children the opportunity to develop good speaking and presentation capabilities.

Having the opportunity to direct one's learning provides feelings of power and control for the child, which contribute positively to his or her sense of competency as a learner (Glasser, 1984). The teacher acts as a facilitator for the child's learning process: power is shared. The teacher does not give up his or her role as the authority, but rather learns to use his or her leadership role in ways that help children develop their own internal behavioral control.

Because the teacher takes into account the children's goals as well as his or her own, there is less potential for conflict. Children can spend more of their time in meaningful learning activity. The more time children spend on instructional tasks, the higher the achievement. Instructional time is lost when teachers have to discipline children who are frustrated or disinterested in classroom activities.

The responsible learner has to develop skill in making productive choices. The integrated classroom offers children many opportunities for choice-making. The integrated classroom, with its multi-age grouping, provides activities, materials, and other resources to accommodate different ability levels, interests, and learning styles. There are no groupings that indicate a hierarchy of ability or that prohibit certain children from participation while inviting others. Children self-select activities and resources that are comfortable for them. The teacher knows the desired outcomes of the learning experience but recognizes that there are any number of ways to achieve the same goals. Because the integrated classroom relies heavily on cooperative group learning, children are not only encouraged to be responsible for their own behavior but to recognize that this responsibility extends to the group.

The child in the integrated classroom works independently within the structure the teacher has established. There are rules and consequences as in any other classroom. Children are encouraged to monitor their own behavior, which encourages them to develop self-control.

The Power Dynamic in the Classroom

Teachers often have difficulty "letting go" of a perceived role that gives them ultimate power over the classroom. Freire writes about the "banking method" of education. He claims that in this method the child is thought of as a passive receptacle which is filled by the teacher. The better the teacher, the more he or she fills the empty container. He explains this concept as follows:

> *Instead of communicating, the teacher issues communiques and makes deposits which the students patiently receive, memorize, and repeat. This is the "banking" concept of education, in which the scope of action allowed to the student extends only as far as receiving, filing, and storing deposits. (Freire, 1990, p. 58)*

Because most teachers have themselves been taught by the banking method of education, it is easily perpetuated. The banking method, in its true form, precludes power sharing with children. It clearly puts all decision-making responsibility on the teacher. It is the teacher's goals that are important, resulting in what the curriculum content should or should not be. If children resist accepting the teacher's goals as their own, pressure is put on them to conform or be punished. Whereas the banking method of education increases the probability that children will take little if any responsibility for their learning, the co-investigation approach, which is a major component of the integrated classroom, does the opposite. Under this approach, the teacher and student plan and learn together, and both have something important to give to the learning process. The co-investigation approach assumes the teacher understands that children can and do construct their own knowledge. It is the child, not the teacher, who abstracts from his or her experiences what is meaningful, and includes this in his or her ever-expanding understanding of the world. Both teacher and child determine the content of learning, and determine how and when this learning will take place. The child becomes an active participant rather than a passive receptacle; the child leads as well as follows. The child develops skills for investigation, learning how to ask questions and then taking responsibility for finding the answers. The teacher becomes the facilitator or coach.

Power and Empowerment

Kreisberg suggests that there are two different types of power; "power over" and "power with." "Power over" is linked with domination; "power with" is the concept of empowerment. Kreisberg defines empowerment as follows:

> *Empowerment is the ability to make a difference, to participate in decision-making, and to take action for change. Empowerment does not assume control of resisting others, but emerges from work with others who are deciding, acting and making a difference. (Kreisberg, 1992, p. xi)*

There is no question that teachers must have control of their classrooms from the perspective that they are ultimately responsible for classroom activity and student outcome. However, there is a difference between being *in control* and being *controlling*. A teacher who is truly in control can relinquish some of his or her power to children, so children also can have some feeling of control over what happens to them. Teachers who are fearful of sharing power tend to make all decisions, use external rewards as a way of controlling behavior, and demand conformity to a predetermined concept of what children should be able to learn as well as how it should be learned.

Ways to Encourage Power Sharing

Children learn to share power, as they learn all knowledge and skills, through actual experience. Often children come to school without any experience in power sharing. They have not had sufficient experience in decision making or problem solving and do not believe that their opinions have any value. When these children have a teacher who wants to share power, they may, at first, feel confused and anxious as to what is expected of them. Because power sharing is a learning process, there have to be many opportunities for success and practice.

Following is a list of ways to share power with children:

1. Deciding *with* children rather than *for* children specific learning content.
2. Giving children choices of activities rather than a predetermined single activity all must do at the same time and in the same way.
3. Determining class rules *with* children rather than setting up the rules *before* children become a part of the classroom.
4. Brainstorming with children possible solutions to problems.
5. Including children in decisions around potential room arrangements.
6. Allowing children to develop their own timetables for completing work projects.
7. Exploring and discussing children's ideas.

8. Encouraging children to work cooperatively in groups and to take leadership responsibility, rather than working in one group with the teacher as the only leader.
9. Encouraging different ways to solve problems, both academic and social.
10. Periodically asking children for their input as to how the classroom is working for them.

Sharing power does not suggest that the teacher abdicate responsibility as an instructional leader, or that there are no pre-set educational goals or outcomes. However, part of the teacher's role as facilitator is to help children understand their individual needs in both the cognitive and social realms. The classroom is a major socializing agent. The child, through this classroom experience, learns how to be a responsible citizen because of many opportunities to share power with adults and peers.

To ensure that children have opportunities to develop a personal sense of power, the teacher must be aware of how power is used in the classroom. Teachers, by the nature of their role, have the power to influence children's behavior in ways that are compatible with the teacher's goals. Influence attempts are the overt manifestations of power. Much classroom conflict is the result of incompatibility between the goals of the teacher and the children, and resulting attempts by the teacher to influence children to give up their goals.

Forms of Power

Raven and French (in Raven and Rubin, 1959) identified five different forms of power that have their basis in the social relationships between two or more individuals. These forms of power give rise to specific influence attempts. Although their work is over thirty years old, much of it is still applicable. They list these powers as: (1) legitimate, (2) expert, (3) referent, (4) coercive, and (5) reward.

Legitimate power relates to the power inherent in the social role of the individual. It requires that others recognize that power role as legitimate. Today's elementary school-age children are not always accepting of the role of the teacher, nor do they always take for granted that the teacher is in charge of the classroom. It is the teacher's responsibility to establish that he or she is in charge, not by intimidation but through knowing when to share power with children and when to give up power to them.

Expert power comes from having particular knowledge that others need. Teachers should be looked upon as having expertise both in subject matter and in procedures that enable children to utilize the classroom environment productively.

Referent power means that others model themselves after or want to be like the person who is attempting to influence their behavior. For elementary school-age children to be influenced by their teachers, they need to recognize these teachers as role models for behavior and values. Teachers may become role models for inappropriate behavior which children mimic with their peers. For instance, when a teacher yells across the room to stop an unwanted action, this often results in children doing the same with other children.

Coercive power and *reward* power appear to be the types of power most frequently used by teachers (Reider, 1989). Compliance with the teacher's goals is most often brought about by giving children happy faces, purple stars, or a special treat or activity for completing work. In lieu of rewards, teachers might use threats or take away activities that are high-priority to children, such as recess, to ensure compliance. When teachers use coercive or reward power, they reduce children's self-directed monitoring and limit their ability to influence except when they are physically present. In order for rewards and coercion to work, children have to care about the reward or be fearful of the punishment. For some children, staying in from recess acts as a reward and only tends to increase the non-compliant behavior. Children in classrooms that are based on coercive and reward power learn little about power sharing and a great deal about manipulation.

Children, like teachers, already have "power." They can refuse to comply with teachers' wishes both verbally and physically. If many children refuse a teacher's attempt at influence simultaneously, they can render the teacher powerless. Some children exert their power by psychologically dropping out of the power dynamic; they stop trying or withdraw altogether, leaving the teacher with little or no ability to influence. When children do not have sufficient opportunities to exert some control (power) over the direction their activity will take, it is easy for them to feel they lack the competency to make things happen for themselves. Purkey and Novak state:

> *It seems self-evident that for students to learn in school, they require sufficient confidence in themselves and their abilities to make some effort to succeed. Self-regard and efforts to control one's destiny correlate highly . . . without self-confidence, students easily succumb to apathy, dependency and loss of self-control. (Purkey and Novak, 1984, p. 29)*

The relationship of shared power to the child's perception of self as competent is clear. The integrated classroom helps children to develop their own goals in concert *with* the teacher rather than in opposition *to* the teacher.

The Development of Competency and Self-Confidence

> *A self-concept is a complex, continuously active system of subjective beliefs about personal existence. It serves to guide behavior and to enable each individual to assume particular roles in life. Rather than initiating activity,*

self-concept serves as a perceptual filter and guides the direction of behavior. . . . In practical classroom situations, students who have learned to see themselves as "schlemiels" are likely to exhibit "schlemiel" behavior. (Purkey and Novak, 1984, p. 39)

Purkey is making an important point about children's behavior when he suggests that self-concepts are not inherited as is eye color. Self-concepts are learned through experiences in interacting with the world. Children's perceptions of themselves as competent learners lead them to act as competent learners, providing more feedback that they are truly good at the learning process. The reverse is true for those children who do not perceive themselves as competent. These are the children who often do not have the confidence to try things on their own or to believe that their ideas are valuable. These children, just like those who perceive themselves as competent, act out their ideas about themselves.

Perceptions of self, once in place, are difficult to change, even when messages about behavior that are inconsistent with the self-concept are received. Individuals rely on self-perception to provide a dependable sense of what to expect from themselves under different circumstances. Many individuals become anxious when perceptions of self are challenged. The tendency is to hold on to perceptions of self even when they are counterproductive. Changing the self-concept is a difficult process. Teachers must recognize that this natural resistance in children makes the process of change slow. For a child to become a responsible learner, he or she needs to perceive the self as competent and capable in the classroom.

All children require what is called *unconditional positive regard.* Everybody needs to feel worthy just because they exist. In addition, certain characteristics that enable the person to be a productive member of his or her society require particular validation. It is our experience that for the responsible learner, these characteristics include:

1. Knowing one's own interests and being motivated to pursue these interests.
2. Being able to work independently on projects.
3. Being able to make choices successfully.
4. Working cooperatively with others.
5. Knowing when to ask for help.
6. Taking responsibility for one's own behavior.

Control and Self-Image: Closely Related

Teachers spend considerable time trying to control what they describe as children's disruptive behavior. For example, teachers become concerned when children are not absorbed with their work, when they annoy their peers, or when they do not follow through with an assignment. When children engage in these behaviors, teachers tell them to pay attention, stop bothering their classmates, or to finish their work. Every time a teacher has to discipline a child, the teacher interrupts the normal flow of activity, and takes time away from instruction, observation of other children, and children's own self-directed learning. Teachers tend to use coercion and rewards in their attempts to get children to stop certain behaviors. And, when all else fails, teachers often resort to threats such as sending the child out to the hall or to the principal. Besides wearing out the teacher, the "disciplined" child is receiving information that he or she is not okay, that his or her behavior is not acceptable, and that he or she is not trying hard enough to conform to expectations. Often teachers' expectations are not realistic. For example, asking a first-grader to sit still and attend to a task in which there is no opportunity for active engagement, is setting the child up for failure, and sending a message that the child is out of control.

Messages that children receive about their behavior become part of their perceptions of self, and these perceptions guide their future behavior. If children perceive that they are out of control, they often feel victimized by their own impulses, and act accordingly. Children who take the position that they are not able to direct their own behavior are going to be children who lack feelings of internal power or competency. As noted previously, feelings of competency are directly related to a positive sense of self, which is the underlying element that supports a child in the learning process. The "I can" attitude necessary for attempting difficult academic tasks, is the same "I can" attitude necessary for the development of self-control. It is not helpful to follow children around dangling prizes or issuing threats to control their behavior. Children need to learn to monitor their own behavior and make conscious decisions regarding their actions. In order for children to develop this "I can" position, they must have opportunities to:

1. Be independent.
2. Make choices and feel these choices are valued.
3. Understand the consequences to behavior.
4. Be able to stop and think about these consequences.
5. Take the responsibility for their own behavior.

It is important for children to say to themselves statements such as, "I can control my actions," "I can make good choices," and "I can stop and think about the consequences of my actions."

To develop self-control, children need to be in classrooms where there are the following characteristics:

1. Rules and consequences that are logical, realistic, and consistently applied. One cannot learn to project consequences if the consequences keep changing.

2. Many opportunities to make choices that support the idea that control over one's life can come from within.

3. A limited and appropriate number of choices so that children do not become overwhelmed.

4. An appropriate amount of auditory and visual stimuli. Too much noise or too many materials or decorations overload the senses making it difficult to stop and think before acting.

5. A sense of order about the classroom. Disorganization tends to increase the child's feeling of being internally chaotic, and makes it more difficult to monitor behavior successfully.

6. A sense of calm. Children's anxieties are raised when teachers appear out of control, which happens when they yell across the room or make threats that frighten children.

7. Children who are actively engaged in classroom tasks. This decreases the probability that they will engage in disruptive behaviors.

8. Classroom procedures that are established *with* children so that expectations are clear.

Motivation and Its Links to Self-Worth

There is an important link between motivation, perceived competency, and the responsible learner. Children can be characterized as having a predominantly internal or external locus of control, meaning that while one child blames someone or something for his or her failures (external), another child perceives that he or she is the one in control of the outcomes of his or her efforts (internal). The first child feels powerless as he or she does not accept responsibility for what happens to him or her, and does not believe that he or she can change the direction of these outcomes. Children who perceive that *they*, rather than something or someone outside themselves, are responsible for outcomes, are more likely to be motivated to engage in tasks, achieving success and increasing positive self-regard (Dembo, 1990).

As children move through the elementary school years, their awareness of how they compare to their peers increases. In the traditional classroom, a child's sense of personal worth is equated with "doing better than" others in the classroom. In classrooms that are competitive by design, there are limited opportunities for all children to excel, encouraging children to "best" each other, and in so doing, demonstrate where they fit into the ability hierarchy. Linking one's sense of worth to the traditional definition of ability is dangerous, according to Martin Covington (Ames and Ames, 1989). He claims perceptions of intellectual adequacy are easily threatened by failure because schools are so "failure-prone." Covington believes that individuals will do what they can to protect their feelings of self-worth, and that they do so by avoiding failure. Children engage in failure avoiding behavior in a number of ways. The most common method of avoiding failure is not to try. Other possibilities range from setting goals so low that failure is almost impossible or setting them so high that failure can easily be blamed on the difficulty of the task. Teachers who encourage children to be realistic about their abilities, and at the same time help children to recognize that effort can increase the probability of achievement, help to make success more attainable. Abilities should be defined in Gardner's terms of multiple intelligences so that there are increased opportunities for success in many areas. In such classrooms, leadership in terms of ability, changes with activities and tasks, providing each child with the chance to excel at something.

If teachers are truly concerned with student motivation, it is important that they examine how much time is spent trying to get children to learn what the teacher thinks is important, and how relevant this material is to the children. This kind of approach does not mean that the teacher has to sacrifice educational goals and outcomes to make learning relevant. In addition, providing rewards and taking away privileges to force a child to engage in activities may actually decrease learning. Some teachers believe that they must always provide a reward or use a threat to get children to engage in a task. Studies have shown that when children are externally rewarded for work that they find intrinsically satisfying, motivation for self-direction decreases (Lepper and Greene, 1978). It is almost as though the child decides that if the teacher has to give a reward, the work must not be as pleasurable or meaningful as originally thought. Good and Brophy (1991) point out that students who are motivated only by grades or other extrinsic rewards are more likely to adopt goals and strategies that concentrate on meeting minimum requirements. Responsible learners must develop their own criteria for evaluating the efforts and outcomes of their work. The child must learn to recognize his or her own accomplishments and value them.

When children are intrinsically motivated to achieve, their learning takes on another form. Csikszentmihalyi uses the term *flow* to describe when involvement in an activity becomes self-sustained and thereby intrinsically motivating. The term *flow* was coined by Csikszentmihalyi after interviews with various individuals about their state of mind when engaged in an activity which provided great pleasure or enjoyment. Often these individuals described the sensation of being carried away as if by a current or "flow" (Benton Center for Curriculum and Instruction, 1990).

Csikszentmihalyi identifies five conditions for flow to occur:

1. Clear goals.
2. Challenges relatively matched with skill level.
3. Immediate feedback.
4. Concentration without the fear of being interrupted.
5. No external time constraints.

At the Key School in Indianapolis, Csikszentmihalyi, along with teachers, is studying his theory of motivation. The Key School, which is based on Gardner's theory of multiple intelligences, is an excellent site for this kind of investigation because the curriculum and structure of the school are designed to engage children in activities of interest and concern to them. The research is designed to address how successful teachers are in creating a learning environment which encourages students to be intrinsically motivated.

Three aspects of the Key School are being investigated. First, a special room has been designed called "The Flow Center." Here, children can utilize a variety of games which correspond to Gardner's seven intelligences. The team of teacher-researchers observes the children as they interact with materials of high interest, recording children's experiences through interviews, questionnaires and videotape, looking for those elements which contribute to the flow. In addition to data collected at the actual Flow Center, data is being collected on how participation in the Center's activities influences children's participation in other school learning experiences. Questions are also being raised as to how the use of school themes as the basis for academic exploration contributes to intrinsic motivation. Children are chosen to attend the Key School by lottery. Researchers are investigating attitudes of children about school and learning, comparing attitudes of those attending the Key School with those of children who wished to attend but were not accepted.

Other research focuses on the relationship between teacher behavior, students' intrinsic motivation, and self-esteem. Deci, Nezlek, and Sheinman (1981) identified two types of teachers, those who are autonomy-oriented and those who are control-oriented in their relationship to students. Autonomy-oriented teachers are more likely to support students in attempts to solve their own problems and pursue their own interests. Control-oriented teachers are more likely to motivate students with rewards and coercion. It was determined that there was a strong positive correlation between the teachers' orientation and students' intrinsic motivation and perceived competence.

The goal, therefore, is to create classrooms where children have experiences that nurture a sense of self as a competent learner, and where children feel they have the ability to achieve and see failure as an indicator that more effort is needed—in other words, that "mistakes" are a normal part of the learning process that can lead to even greater accomplishment. Children should feel that making a mistake is not something horrible to fear, but rather something that can lead to greater understanding and learning.

Such a classroom of 6-, 7-, and 8-year-olds exists in the Santa Fe public school system. The teacher is a veteran of teaching single-age primary classes over a period of fifteen years. Her observations over the years led to her firm conviction that these single-age groupings did not work effectively for all children. Each year she had some children at risk for failure in the next grade who did not, however, need retention in the one just completed.

Reading, careful study, and research gave the teacher the background she needed to plan and organize for a multi-age classroom of 6-, 7-, and 8-year-olds. The physical environment she created gave clear messages to the children about what was there in the way of materials, and suggested appropriate activities for the children to pursue. The teacher became the catalyst, coach, resource and, when appropriate and needed, a teacher in classical terms as well as a sensitive observer of children.

This classroom supports the idea that *all children can learn* and that each child is responsible for his or her own learning and behavior. Children make choices about when and where they will work, and guided choices about what they will pursue. Class projects built around theme studies provide small and large group interactions and provide children with choices of topics and, frequently, work partners. There is no failure in this classroom, only different degrees of success. The children in this classroom, over the few years of its existence, have demonstrated not only their ability to make appropriate choices and solve their own disputes (which are infrequent), but also that they have met the state competencies in academic areas earlier than most.

Children in this classroom are not afraid of making mistakes or not meeting goals. Each child plans with the teacher weekly to meet specific objectives via a wide variety of open-ended contracts. Rules are few and are based on common courtesy and mutual respect; consequences for breaking these rules are clear and followed through on consistently. Assessment is ongoing. It is built into contracts and is accomplished by both child and teacher on a weekly basis.

The environment supports the children and teacher by providing, for children, developmentally appropriate materials and suggested tasks, and, for the teacher, freedom to work with individuals or small groups of children. But while the environment is rich with resources, no workspace looks visually busy. Children's work is posted everywhere, obviously displayed neatly and proudly by the children themselves. Each child's work is unique: twenty-five papers exhibiting identical spelling words are *not* part of these displays.

Work groups are formed sometimes by friendships, but more frequently by a wide range of individuals with linguistic, logical-mathematical, spatial, bodily-kinesthetic, musical, and intra- and interpersonal intelligences. Sometimes combinations are formed depending on the research and skills needed to complete the project. Children are never grouped by so-called age or grade designations: 6-, 7-, and 8-year-olds interact, learn and teach, help and guide, model, and imitate.

Parents are an active and enthusiastic part of this classroom. The teacher calls each one at the beginning of the year, asking how each can and might wish to contribute, recognizing that some parents are not available to participate directly in classroom activities. Some parents may contribute by providing materials or chaperoning field trips. Other parents may volunteer in the classroom. Parent volunteers are taught how to work effectively in this classroom and add another dimension to the real-world environment. The result is truly the establishment of a "community of learners."

Multi-Age Groupings: Relationship to Responsible Learning

The classroom cited in the previous section utilizes multi-age grouping. This supports a closer, more sensitive relationship between student and teacher as the child remains in the same classroom over the three-year age range. The teacher can then become well-acquainted with the child, his or her learning style, and his or her behavioral needs. The teacher can provide an environment which is supportive of the development of positive self-concepts as well as cognitive growth. Children benefit from this longer span of time with one teacher because they can get to know that teacher well. In the single-age classroom structure that moves children to another teacher every year, some children lose momentum because they are moved just when they were getting to feel comfortable with a particular teacher and set of classroom expectations. Some children take a considerable length of time in a particular classroom to even feel comfortable enough to speak out. Multi-age groupings can help this type of shyness without wasting a major part of the year: once a child becomes comfortable, the child can and often does make gigantic strides in his or her academic work.

The integrated classroom resembles the real world in both physical setup and the use of an integrated, problem-solving approach to learning. Another way in which it resembles the real world is in including children of multiple ages. Children do not live in environments comprised entirely of people exactly their age; there are often older and younger siblings in their households and within neighboring families. Neighborhoods, communities, and streets include people of many ages. In the integrated classroom, children interact on a daily basis with older and younger children, learning the intricate and important skills of negotiating the social world. For the elementary school-age child, being socially competent is a major contributor to a positive self-concept. Socially competent behavior also allows children to resolve interpersonal conflicts independently, adding to the children's feelings of being in control of their behavior, and, therefore, their world.

Multi-age groupings contribute to the cognitive as well as the social-emotional growth of the children. British teachers, as they created the model over fifty years ago, realized that one teacher could not possibly work with each child on a one-to-one basis if all children in the group were at similar ages and stages, each making like demands on the teacher as a singular age-stage group tends to do. British teachers were also aware that forty 6-year-olds, all school beginners, are not all ready for the same presentation of a concept or skill at precisely the same time or in the same way. This holds true for older children as well, whose differences in learning styles and in readiness for specific concepts grow wider over the years rather than narrower. Multi-age groupings were then and are now seen as a way of capitalizing on the benefits of peer coaching and teaching. Teachers attest to the ability of children to help and teach each other, often in a way more acceptable and understandable than that of the teacher with a whole group. Opportunities for academic success are increased with appropriate activities and a multitude of "teachers," in peers as well as the official teacher. Because the multi-age classroom becomes a community of teachers and learners, the teacher's load is not increased as many suppose, but broadened. He or she can take time to give children specific feedback about their behavior, help children to solve conflicts, and assist children in identifying constructive ways of getting their needs met.

There are major arguments concerning what age ranges should be used for multi-age classrooms. The previously cited public school classroom in Santa Fe, New Mexico, utilizes a combination of children 6, 7, and 8 years old. This works well for this experienced teacher. However, using Piaget's theories and the British example as our guide, we can conclude that children whose thinking is basically within the same stage of development should be grouped together. In other words, the preoperational thinkers belong together and the concrete operational thinkers belong together. In terms of school ages, this usually means that the 5-, 6-, and 7-year-olds belong in a group, and the 8-, 9-, and 10-year-olds belong together in another group. If it is an elementary school with kindergarten through grade six, then grade six (the 11-year-olds) belong in a group by themselves, as they are transitioning to the stage of formal operation. A three-year age span is and has been considered ideal in most integrated, multi-age classrooms. There needs to be enough difference in concept, understanding, and skills development as well as in social-emotional levels to have children become truly independent and responsible learners. Greater age ranges result in *not* being able to create an environment that meets needs appropriately; some children are always being left out. Two-year age spans do not give enough variety to allow for effective peer coaching and modeling.

Teacher Behaviors that Support the Responsible Learner

Teachers communicate through *how* they say something as well as through *what* it is they're saying. Children are good at picking up cues from adults through listening not just to words but to tone and inflection. Children read adult behavior by watching facial expressions and body movements. Through both verbal and nonverbal communication, the teacher conveys to the child his or her perceptions of the child's academic and social competency. Because verbal and nonverbal behaviors are not always congruent, children get mixed messages about their behavior and the teacher's expectations for performance.

It is likely that a child will select the nonverbal cues coming from the teacher before the verbal information if there is a discrepancy between the two. For example, a teacher might say to a child upon arrival in the classroom "I'm really glad you are here today, Billy. The other children want you to help construct our store." The words are fine. They suggest that Billy is a valued member of the group and that he has expertise that can add to a class project. The nonverbal behavior states something else. With arms across chest, with eyes averted, and a tightness around the mouth, the teacher conveys a state of unhappiness at seeing Billy, and possibly a concern that once he joins the group, problems will occur.

For children to become responsible learners, they need specific verbal and nonverbal feedback from the teacher about their ongoing contributions. Listening with the body by getting down to the child's eye level, and leaning towards the child when speaking indicate to the child that what he or she has to say is valuable and important. Staying with the child while talking and keeping eyes focused on the child rather than on other things happening in the room communicates to the child the teacher's interest. Saying things that reinforce a positive sense of self may include statements such as, "I am really interested in your ideas," "I enjoy working with you on this project," "You made good choices about the resources that you needed," and "That was great the way you helped Susan with that problem." Making certain that statements give children feedback about their own internal locus of control addresses the effort and ability that the child has demonstrated, as well as the child's competency at solving problems and negotiating conflicts. When children know exactly what they did well, they can repeat the behavior and make conscious choices regarding actions and outcomes.

Children who are struggling with tasks need *accurate* feedback along with encouragement. Teachers, in their attempts to raise children's self-esteem, will often praise children for their effort or for whatever outcome they produce. Elementary school-age children are well aware when they are not doing as well as their peers. When children believe that teachers are not realistic in their praise, they may conclude that the teacher feels sorry for them and has low expectations for what they can produce. Children who perceive that the teacher does not believe they are capable will often live up to this expectation. As stated by Rachel (age 10): "My teacher does not like kids. She gives directions to the whole class and she won't answer questions if we misunderstand. She makes kids feel dumb. My teacher is ready for us to be bad. She doesn't like me or my friend. She yells a lot at kids but makes them speak quietly!" Jessica (age 11), however, responds to a different set of expectations. She is more likely to go beyond her initial perceptions of herself as a learner to meet the expectations of the teacher: "I like my teacher a lot. She encourages me to do harder stuff. She also listens to me. She wants you to express your feelings and be in charge of your own behavior."

Children are extremely sensitive to the messages that teachers send both by words and actions. If teachers want children to develop self-responsibility and a sense of self-worth as learners, they must approach the classroom with a willingness to listen carefully to what children say. They must also find ways of monitoring their own nonverbal behavior, perhaps with the use of a video camera.

Suggested Activities

1. Often teachers realize that they are inconsistent in what they consider to be acceptable behavior, depending upon their personal reactions to an individual child. For example, one child who speaks his or her mind in a playful way may find that the teacher listens and even laughs, while another child who speaks his or her mind in a more direct manner may find the teacher critical, which suggests that the behavior is disrespectful. To help a teacher become more consistent in his or her expectations and responses to behavior, the following exercise is suggested:

Take a sheet of paper and divide it in half. On the left half of the paper, write all the behaviors you usually find acceptable in children. On the right side of the paper, write those behaviors you usually find unacceptable. Write down some of the ways you respond to acceptable behavior. Make a list of positive comments that give children specific information so that they can be more conscious of including these behaviors in their repertoire. Now write down some ways in which you usually respond to unacceptable behavior. Determine what you would like to change in these responses, writing down more positive and specific responses. By doing this exercise, you can develop your awareness of what behaviors are acceptable and unacceptable, independent of the child who performs them. When your responses to these behaviors become more consistent, children can rely on certain expectations and certain consequences, enabling them to predict outcomes and monitor their behavior. In addition, children begin to understand that it is a particular behavior that is the problem, and not them.

2. Sometimes when behavior that is ordinarily acceptable seems unacceptable in a particular child, the teacher might need to gain more information about the child and his or her relationship to the child. Trying to look at the child in a new light requires asking certain questions:

a. In what stage of development is the child?
b. Are some of the unacceptable behaviors really typical of children at this stage?
c. Are activities too difficult or too easy for this child?
d. Does the child feel accepted by you? How do you know?
e. Is the child reacting to feelings of rejection or not being liked? What makes you think so?

   3. Teachers often keep journals which reflect their classroom experiences. A journal or log of your responses to children can be a helpful tool in providing perspective and insight into how you feel about different children. The trick in keeping such a journal or log, is not to be critical of what you are saying. This is your opportunity to say whatever you want about a child, even if it is something very negative. On one side of the page you write these personal comments which are just as you feel them, without any censorship. On the other side of the page you write what you believe to be a suitable, professional response. This exercise can provide some objectivity without negating your very real and important feelings.

   4. A good way of determining whether you are encouraging a responsible learner is to ask yourself the following questions:

a. Do children have appropriate choices?
b. Do you give children opportunities to figure out the answers to both academic and social problems with only enough assistance to facilitate the problem solving?
c. Do you give specific feedback, such as saying to a child, "I particularly like the way you described the wagon in your story; you did not just say 'wagon' but used its correct name, 'Conestoga wagon,' as well as descriptive words that really made me see a Conestoga wagon in my mind."
d. Do you ask children to tell you what they like about what they are doing, so that they can develop a greater awareness of what they feel is valuable and important? For example, a teacher in a multi-age primary class asked a child just coming to literacy, "What words do you want to learn today?" The child responded, "I want to learn *yellow, red,* and *blue.*" The teacher asked why he chose those words. He responded that they are his favorite colors. This child is much more likely to retain his chosen words than words selected by the teacher.

   5. An interesting way to conceptualize the interrelationship between the components that contribute to the responsible learner is shown in a diagram

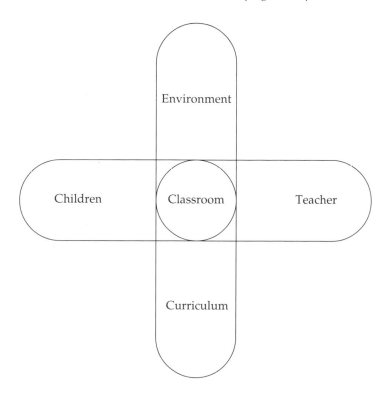

presented by Dr. Kathy Nelson to her preservice class of elementary education majors at the College of Santa Fe.

In this diagram, Dr. Nelson captured the interlocking nature of the different pieces which influence the development of the responsible learner. Each piece impacts on all of the other pieces. The support for the responsible learner comes from these pieces working in harmony to provide the necessary scaffolding for the child. To assist students in understanding the components that influence the responsible learner, Dr. Nelson presented the following six lists:

The Responsible Learner

- Active participant not a passive receptacle
- Self-directed
- Intrinsically motivated
- Risk-taker
- Personal sense of power
- Uses time wisely
- Succeeds
- Works independently within structure established
- Usually behaves but understands consequences when problem arises

The Teacher of Responsible Learners

- Avoids using external control/power
- Shares power
- Is a facilitator or coach
- Uses leadership role to help children develop their own internal behavior control
- Takes into account children's goals as well as their own
- In control rather than controlling
- Helps children understand their cognitive and social needs

Self-Concept

- Self-esteem: seeing oneself as a valued, productive member of a group who:

  1. has interests.
  2. is independent.
  3. makes choices.
  4. cooperates.
  5. controls behavior.
  6. can get help when needed.

- Universal need for unconditional positive regard
- Learned from experience
- Impact of teacher

  1. Environment
  2. Curriculum
  3. Teaching social skills

     - Identifying problems
     - Brainstorm solutions/actions
     - Try out solutions/actions
     - Assess/evaluate

  4. Teacher's own interpersonal skills—messages (verbal and nonverbal)

Four Kinds of Power

1. Legitimate (because of social role)
2. Expert (knowledge needed by others)
3. Referent (messages sent by modeling)
4. Manipulative (coercion and reward/punishment)

Child without Power

- May quit trying
- Refuses to comply

- Drops out
- Develops an external locus of control

Curriculum that Encourages Responsible Learners

- Allows productive choices and self-selection
- Lots of child-directed learning
- Based on interests
- Within the parameters of teacher's and community's goals
- Emphasizes process but still values product
- Accomodates different abilities, interests, and learning styles
- Allows many ways to achieve the same goal
- Promotes cooperation and concern for the group
- Uses a co-investigative approach (not banking)

Students were asked to identify specific actions that demonstrate each of the items on the lists. This was done to help students understand more clearly the specific elements that need to be considered. This is a strongly recommended activity for anyone who wants more clarity as to the development of the responsible learner.

6. What's wrong with this scenario? Lynn teaches a kindergarten through second grade primary classroom. Frank is 5 years old, but big for his age. His parents and his teacher tend to treat him as though he were older. When he does something they do not like, he is told to act his age. Frank also has three older brothers and tends to mimic their aggressive behavior, which takes the form of hitting or pushing other children who get in his way. Lynn is upset with Frank because he will not sit and attend for as long as other boys in the class. In addition, his aggressive ways of solving conflicts with his peers is particularly disturbing. Frank tries to sit on Lynn's lap when she reads stories to the group. Lynn finds this inappropriate even though other children find their way onto her lap without difficulty. One day, Frank ran from one end of the Lynn's classroom to the other where Lynn was talking to another boy about Frank's age. Frank ran headfirst into Lynn's stomach, and when Lynn displayed both pain and anger, Frank just laughed.

What do you think Lynn could have done differently to avoid this kind of confrontation with Frank? What do you think Frank was feeling in regard to his relationship with his teacher? Why? What was Frank trying to tell Lynn by his behavior when he ran into her stomach?

7. Children often have difficulties resolving conflicts without a great deal of teacher intervention because they don't really know how to identify the real issue or issues. For example, two children might be struggling over who will use a particular piece of equipment first. When asked by the teacher to define the problem, each one replies that he or she had it first. The real issue is that there is one piece of equipment, and both children require its use to complete their projects. The children can be helped by the teacher to:

a. identify the *real* issue.
b. brainstorm without evaluation possible alternative solutions that are agreeable to both children.
c. decide on which solution or idea to try first.
d. determine a time line for assessing the success of the solution or idea.

This process can be used in academic problem-solving situations as well as in social ones.

References

Ames, Russell E. and Ames, Carole. (1984). *Motivation in Education.* Florida: Academic Press.

Benton Center for Curriculum and Instruction. (1990). Report from the Center. Chicago: University of Chicago. 3 (1).

Brendtro, Larry, Broken Leg, Martin, and Van Bockern, Steve. (1990). *Reclaiming Youth at Risk.* Indiana: National Educational Service.

Deci, E. L., Nezlek, J., and Sheinman, L. (1981). Characteristics of the Rewarder and Intrinsic Motivation of the Rewardee. *Journal of Personality and Social Psychology.*

Dembo, Myron H. (1991). *Applying Educational Psychology in the Classroom.* New York: Longman.

Freire, Paulo. (1990). *Pedagogy of the Oppressed.* New York: The Continuum Press.

Glasser, William. (1984). *Control Theory.* New York: Harper and Row Publishers.

Good, Thomas and Brophy, Jere. (1991). *Looking in Classrooms.* New York: Harper Collins.

Kreisberg, Seth. (1992). *Transforming Power.* New York: State University of New York Press.

Lepper, M. R. and Greene, D. (1978). *The Hidden Cost of Rewards.* New Jersey: Erlbaum.

Purkey, William and Novak, John. (1984). *Inviting School Success.* California: Wadsworth.

Raven, Bertram and Rubin, Jeffrey. (1983). *Social Psychology.* New York: John Wiley and Sons.

Reider, Barbara. (1989). *The Relationship of Teachers' Uses of Influence and Children's Responses.* Unpublished dissertation.

5

Assessment: Formal and Informal

It makes sense to think of human competence as an emerging capacity, one likely to be manifest at the intersection of three different constituents: the "individual," with his or her skills, knowledge and aims: the structure of a "domain of knowledge," within which these skills can be aroused; and a set of institutions and roles—a surrounding "field"—which judges when a particular performance is acceptable and when it fails to meet specifications. (Gardner, 1993, p. 172-173)

The strength of the integrated classroom as a learning environment for children is contingent upon the teacher knowing children as individuals; their strengths in terms of intelligences, their areas of weakness, their interests, and their relationships with peers and adults. "Knowing" children requires that the teacher develop skills as an observer of children's activities, and the competencies involved in recording and interpreting these observations. Because children in the integrated classroom spend so much of their time in interaction with others, listening is a major component of observation. The ongoing assessment process inherent in the integrated approach provides the data that the teacher uses for planning and for evaluating outcomes. It focuses on the individual child, not just in terms of what he or she knows, but also on what the child is in the process of knowing. Without this form of assessment, classroom activity becomes a far less meaningful exercise in which children do things without clear direction as to why. Assessment for the integrated classroom, in many respects, looks different than that of a more traditional classroom. The tools that are used for data collection, and the teacher's role as observer, change given the goals of this type of classroom.

A Window into Two Classrooms

Classroom 1: An Integrated Classroom of Children 8, 9 and 10 Years Olds

As happens frequently in this classroom, the teacher is observing the children while they are actively engaged in a project. The project they are currently working on is on architecture. Some are working alone, some are in pairs and threes, and there is also one group of four sharing what they have just finished researching on early colonial styles of houses. There are materials everywhere: books, posters, pamphlets, picture files, and art supplies of all kinds as well as boxes of junk materials for creating scale houses and furniture.

Because of the active involvement of all the children, the teacher can move easily from child to child and group to group, making notes, asking questions, and assessing cooperative work habits, as well as making suggestions for further extension of the investigation. Mr. Jones also is observing carefully learning strategies and styles, noting specific strengths of individual children. He listens closely for about ten minutes to the cooperative group discussion, again noting where they might need specific help on creating an accurate scale floor plan of a seventeenth century New England house.

At the end of the day, the teacher enters amd notes what he has observed on specific children in the large notebook he keeps on the children in his class. This notebook is set up with a section for each child and contains not only observational notes, but also specific goals and objectives or plans that he wants to keep uppermost in his mind for each child as the theme study progresses.

As Mr. Jones scans the pages and previous entries for his class, he makes particular note of those children on whom there has not been an observation this week so that he can focus specifically on them tomorrow. Indications are that everything is working just fine for these four children; however, he must be sure.

Classroom 2: A Traditional Classroom

In this classroom, the teacher is sitting quietly at her desk grading the practice pages from the arithmetic workbook the children handed in this morning. The class, meanwhile, is reading the assignment in the science text and answering the questions at the end of the chapter.

The major method of assessment, here, is grading, with the score for each worksheet or paper carefully entered in a grade book. By spending time at her desk grading papers while children are "working," this teacher misses many opportunities to observe children in the learning process. Because she grades only the final product, Mrs. Smith does not know if Susy is subtracting by borrowing or by adding backwards. She cannot know if Johnny is spelling so well because he is sounding out each syllable, or if he has an incredible visual memory. Her assessment of Sara lets her think that Sara really does not study or apply herself: she makes so many errors on her math homework. Actually, Sara is really a gifted mathematician; her thinking processes show insight, solid reasoning, and creative problem solving. Sara's problem lies with arithmetic practice: she knows the process and can estimate the answer quickly and reasonably—she becomes bored with the endless number of practice problems assigned each night. Because Mrs. Smith has never talked at length with Sara, or asked her how she arrived at her answers, her assessment of Sara is solely a string of scores in her grade book: 61, 69, 52, 98, 43, 59, 64. That "98" affirms for Mrs. Smith that she is correct in her assessment—if only Sara tried harder more often!

Mrs. Smith makes up her lesson plans for tomorrow from the teacher's guide for each textbook used. Doesn't it make sense to follow the curriculum guides? Don't the publishers know best what should come next? In this classroom, the major time for social interaction is on the playground, and the teacher is "on duty" only about every two weeks. She is not able to observe how children interact informally around issues not related to academics.

This teacher does not have a good sense of the "whole child." To her, the child is primarily a cognitive being represented by test scores and daily worksheets. Therefore, her ability to plan for each child as an individual is severely limited. In addition, the focus of the classroom does not address the social aspect of learning, nor does it support how individual children display their unique intelligences.

Assessment: A Definition of Terms

Assessment in the integrated classroom includes observation of children, the collection of information regarding different aspects of children's interactions within the total environment, the analysis of this data, and the utilization of this analysis for future planning. The teacher needs to have knowledge about children that goes beyond what can be obtained using the unilateral standardized method, otherwise known as "teach and test." This does not mean that formal assessment isn't an important component of the assessment process. However, formal testing does not provide enough information about how individual children think and process concepts, how they assess their own learning, and how they utilize their inter- and intrapersonal intelligences. The integrated classroom approach relies on a totally different level of understanding children. It takes into account their cognitive and social development, and the strengths and combinations of the various intelligences.

Observation: The Basic Component of Assessment

Careful observation of children as they work on tasks and interact with each other provides the teacher with data to assist in planning curriculum and evaluating student progress. Being a good "kid-watcher" (Goodman and Goodman, 1978) is particularly important in the integrated classroom where accurate assessment of children's developmental level is the basis for teacher decisions. Being a "kid-watcher" requires that the teacher simply be a careful, sensitive, and focused observer of children in order to support accurate assessment. Without this assessment, teachers are unable to design an environment or provide choices of activities which help to ensure student success and continued growth. Through observation, teachers can validate hunches and assumptions they make concerning a child's approach to certain learning tasks or a child's relationship to his or her peers. Observation also helps to locate problem areas which can include problems in the environment, the curriculum, teacher/child relationships, child/child relationships or instructional strategies.

Skills for Effective Observation

Being a good observer requires skill and practice. Specific skills for effective observation of children's interactions with peers, classroom materials, and adults as well as their general ways of approaching the learning environment include:

1. an understanding of development.
2. the ability to focus on relevant information.
3. knowing what can be observed in a particular setting.
4. knowing how to be objective.
5. knowing what is important to record.
6. using language appropriately to describe the observation.
7. knowing how to categorize observations.
8. knowing how to look for patterns in observations.
9. knowing how to make inferences.
10. knowing what observation tools to use.
11. knowing how to listen to what children say.

Without an understanding of development, it is difficult to interpret the meaning of observed behavior. Developmental theory guides the teacher in assessing a child's readiness for specific learning experiences and helps him or her make decisions regarding modifications in the environment or curriculum. A teacher in a first grade class was doing visual-spatial problem solving using two-inch paper squares and a shape drawn on geoboard paper as shown below:

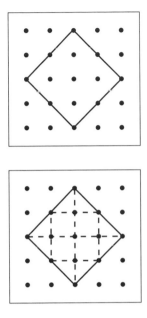

The children had no problem placing the whole squares, and even the half-squares needed at the top of the shape. Several children, however, had great difficulty placing the half-squares on the right and left sides as well as at the bottom of the shape. Even with cues from the teacher, these same few children quickly removed the correct placement they had just made with their teacher's help, and returned to using their own interpretation of the instructions. It became obvious to the teacher that they did not yet have the perceptual ability to either rotate the design or to "see" that the sides and bottom were identical to the top. The teacher then modified the lesson to allow for more exploration and discovery, at different levels of sophistication, of how different pieces fit within the whole.

Useful observations are focused. A focused observation requires the teacher to have a purpose in mind as to the kind of information that he or she wishes to gather. For example, a teacher may want information about the quality of play between a particular child and his peers. The teacher may focus his or her observation to answer such questions as: (1) how successful is this child in communicating his ideas to his peers? (2) what role does the child take in the play situation? and (3) how does the child resolve conflicts when they arise? If the teacher is unclear as to the purpose of the observation, it is difficult to weed out irrelevant data. Rather than come away with useful information, the teacher comes away with a hodgepodge of data that may provide few, if any, guidelines for teacher decision making. The less focused the teacher, the more likely it is that important information will be lost or distorted. Sometimes the teacher decides to watch and listen, with the idea that some important information may be obtained. This is a critical first step in the observation process. From these initial experiences, the teacher may begin to formulate questions that guide future observations.

Particular behaviors and interactions will occur in certain settings and not in others. For example, a teacher has suspicions that a particular child who works well in pairs or by herself is the cause of group discord when placed with four or five children. The teacher creates a group brainstorming session with specified children. She is really more interested in watching and listening to this child interact with peers than she is in the ideas flowing from the group. She can put a tape recorder on the table to catch the brainstorming ideas for later listening, so she will not be distracted from the focus of her observation.

It is similarly important for the teacher to create learning experiences that allow for specific demonstrations of competence and knowledge. If, for example, a teacher wants to observe how a child uses concepts and skills across content areas and with genuine understanding, he or she needs to design tasks or projects that will evoke the practical use of such concepts and skills. Along with focusing observations, the teacher must carefully plan the setting and the experiences.

Objective observation provides the teacher with information that takes the observed actions out of the realm of opinion and puts it into context. Being objective requires recognition of one's own biases and preferred ways of observing. Inherent in biases are value systems, personal likes and dislikes, and responses to certain types of actions. For example, Harry becomes angry when he feels the teacher is unfair. He tells the teacher that he thinks he is mean and that he hates him because he doesn't see or listen to his side of the story. The teacher believes that Harry is just stubborn and wrongfully questioning his authority. Another teacher might interpret Harry's behavior quite differently based on a different value system. This teacher, unlike the first, believes children should stand up for themselves, even to adults. She considers Harry's remarks to be informative and begins to reflect on her classroom expectations. What one teacher views as a problem, another teacher views as a strength.

Teachers come to their classrooms with histories that color their perceptions of children, and of themselves. Objective observations require the teacher to collect data without imposing his or her values, impressions, or conclusions. Being objective is very difficult; it is easy to interpret observations by jumping to conclusions and putting closure on the observation before all the information is known. Objective observations are fact-finding.

They require teachers to gather data over a period of time without making judgments. When enough data is collected, the teacher reviews it for patterns that suggest that what he or she observed has in fact occurred, and has not been colored with personal opinion.

Individuals have preferred ways of observing what is happening around them. Some are attracted to details; they will notice the kind of clothes someone is wearing, how often the other person looks at them, and whether it is sunny or cloudy. Other people are more global in their observations; they may not be able to remember the time of day, the person's dress, or exactly what the other person said, but can easily describe a general impression. The first group of people may be particularly good at quantifying observations, and may need to work harder at qualitatively describing what they see. The second group may need to learn how to detail what they have seen. Both groups may be excellent observers; however, the focus of an observation should determine the approach, not the teacher's personal preference. If the focus of an observation is to determine how many different children a particular child addresses in an hour, quantifying is important. If the issue is *how* the child addresses other children, the number of children the child addresses may be less important and counting them can be distracting to the observer.

Initially, teachers need to document observations in great detail. By highlighting specific information, the teacher begins to identify patterns, problems, and strengths. Frequent observations of children help the teacher focus on the kinds of information they want and need for present and future planning. Scripting what children actually say, following a child around describing specific actions, and detailing the setting provide accurate material for reflection and consideration. Through this reflection, the teacher can sift out irrelevant information, and keep what is pertinent to the focus.

As teachers observe and describe what they see and hear, it is important that they look for words that capture the nuances of the situation. Describing Billy's approach to a task, one teacher might say that Billy moves hesitantly towards the workspace containing mathematics manipulatives. When at the workspace, he haphazardly picks up several unrelated items that cannot possibly help him solve the stated problem. He begins to playfully build with the pieces, talking to himself about skyscrapers. This description provides a different sense of Billy than one that simply says that Billy plays with the materials rather than getting down to work.

Eventually, the teacher must draw some conclusion from observations. If observations are made over a period of time, patterns become evident. The child who never seems to pay attention may only become distracted before lunch. Making certain that this child has a midmorning snack may be all that is needed to help this child stay focused for the rest of the morning. Having a variety of representations of the child's behavior or working strategies keeps the teacher from drawing conclusions from inadequate sources of information.

Sometimes teachers draw inaccurate conclusions because they are more inexperienced in inferring from their observations. A teacher cannot get inside a child's head to understand exactly how a child is approaching a problem. However, listening accurately to a child talk about what he or she is doing allows the teacher to infer particular strategies. A child who is unwilling to take risks and often makes demeaning statements about his or her competencies may in fact have a poor self-image. The teacher must know that these behaviors are indicative of this internal vision in order to make this assumption.

Ways of Collecting Information: The Assessment Process

Besides being direct observers, teachers have to be attentive listeners and skillful questioners. Depending on the kinds of information the teacher needs to acquire, examples of data and data collection tools include:

1. student products
2. student processfolios and portfolios
3. performance assessment
4. interviews
5. student self-assessment
6. audio- and videotapes
7. checklists
8. frequency charts
9. who-to-whom charts
10. running records
11. anecdotal records
12. teacher self-evaluation
13. student evaluations of classroom and teacher

Teachers want to know: (1) how a child thinks, (2) what information the child already has, (3) how the child chooses to exhibit this information, (4) whether the child can generalize from specific examples to more broadly-based concepts, (5) whether the child's social skills are appropriate to the child's age and developmental level, (6) whether the child takes risks, (7) the child's strengths and preferred ways of learning, (8) the child's motivation and sense of responsibility for learning, (9) the child's planning and organizational abilities, (10) the level of skills, and what skill areas, the child has developed, and (11) how the child feels about him- or herself as a learner.

Teachers must be concerned with time management. It always is not possible for a teacher to physically remove him- or herself from the class to do an observation. Selecting the data collection tools appropriate for the information needed is an important aspect of planning. Teachers also should recognize that the gathering of information and the final recording of this information are not necessarily the same. For example, a child's written work may be considered a source of data. It also provides a written record of sorts. However, the teacher at some point probably will write a narrative description of this written work including inferences and recommendations for how the information gathered can be used to assist the child. The final recording of information may be used by the teacher for an overall assessment of the child's progress in the classroom, for communication with parents or other professionals, or as a guide for writing student records that may become part of the child's permanent record. It is important for teachers to consider carefully how they write these final reports. Issues of objectivity, use of language, and confidentiality all become critical. Any data collected should be kept in spaces not accessible to anyone except authorized personnel. Teachers' notes may include subjective information that the teacher can sift through accurately. This information, however, should not be identified as "fact."

Informal Data Collection Tools

Student Products

The ways of assessing student products may be as varied as the products themselves. The "product" may be a singular piece of work in any subject area, or a product that evolves from an integrated project which crosses content areas. The product may be something written, a piece of artwork, a chart or a graph, a piece of music, a play, a demonstration, or another kind of performance. In one third-, fourth-, and fifth-grade classroom a group of children demonstrated their knowledge of pollution caused by oil spills. The group researched the Valdes oil spill as well as others that had happened around the same time. The children were concerned particularly with the methods used to clean up and the ultimate outcome of this endeavor. They made a model of an oil spill by placing oil in a large pan of water. They then gathered a variety of materials to be used in removing the spill. They also found bird feathers to put into the spill in order to test the effects of oil on birds and the possibility of removing the oil. They found that some clean-up methods worked better than others, but that it was impossible to return water to its former purity. The bird feathers were very difficult to clean and gave the children a clear understanding of the magnitude of the problem facing those that gathered to save the water fowl in the Valdes area. The children found that they were left with cleaner water but also with all of the clean-up materials, which posed an eco-logical problem in itself. The children recorded their work in multiple ways. As a result of this project, the children decided that they wanted to commit to a weekly clean-up of their school grounds as a way of contributing to a more ecologically sound environment. They also decided to start a recycling project. Over the course of the project on oil spills, the teacher observed and interacted with individuals as well as the group, listening to and recording information about how individual children were learning. The data the teacher recorded included:

1. individual child's skills in researching.
2. how well each child was able to move from the concrete to the abstract concept of pollution problems.
3. cooperative skills in accomplishing the project.
4. children's skills in presenting the project, including written work, charts, graphs, and drawings, as well as oral reports.
5. children's ability to project possible solutions and plan for them.
6. the effect of the project on future learning.

Processfolios and Portfolios

A *processfolio* is a collection of a child's work from first ideas and initial plan-ning through the completion of the finished product. It should include all manner of scrap-paper ideas, drawings, and so forth. According to Howard Gardner (1993), an evaluation of a child's thinking can occur accurately only if the teacher has followed the progression of thinking from its inception.

> *In a standard portfolio, an individual collects his or her best work, prelim-inary to some kind of competition or exhibition. As a contrast, in a process-folio, the student deliberately attempts to document—for himself as well as for others—the rocky road to his involvement in a project: the initial plans, the interim sketches, the false starts, the pivotal turning point, objects from the domain that are relevant and that he likes or dislikes, various forms of interim and final evaluations, and plans for new and subsequent projects. (Wolf et al., 1991, in Gardner, 1993, p. 225)*

The "inquiry" approach to learning, in which children are encouraged first to formulate the problem then plan for solving it, is a good example of the use of a processfolio.

A *portfolio*, in contrast to a processfolio, contains samples of a variety of fin-ished products, chosen by both the student and the teacher as exemplary work over a given period of time. The choices that teachers and children make about what should be put into the portfolio is a good indication of what is valued. If a portfolio is going to be assessed by individuals other than the teacher, such

A Third-, Fourth-, Fifth-Grade Classroom
in Rural New Mexico

Reuben was part of a small group whose task it was to choose a question to investigate about the early Spanish settlers in northern New Mexico. Their readings into background history led them to wonder what games were played and what toys were used by the children of these settlers. The first entry into Reuben's personal journal was documentation of his initial readings, and the questions that came from these readings. The next journal entry contained a summary of the group's discussion of individual questions, and Reuben's perception of why a particular question was agreed upon. Reuben found other questions more interesting to him personally, and made a note to himself about following up on these later. In addition, Reuben made a list for himself of what specific areas of the games/toys question he wanted to follow and why. As the project unfolded, each of the children added drawings, stories, descriptions, and personal opinions as to the relevance of these games and toys to children today. Each child's specific part of the study added another piece to the overall understanding of the lifestyle and hardships of these pioneers. In addition, each child's personal journal reflected his or her reactions to these toys and games. Since many of the children in this classroom are themselves of Spanish descent, they were able to add personal anecdotes as well as sample toys from grandparents and great grandparents. The final "products," which were the children's individual processfolios, reflected many ways of learning as well as many ways of representing what they had learned, including some video presentations. In addition, the teacher and each child were able to look back at those questions and concerns that were important for that child: where he or she had problems, why the child had changed his or her mind about pursuing specific items, the first rough sketches and drafts, and so forth. All processfolio items were carefully dated, and put into chronological order for more accurate assessment. From his processfolio, Reuben learned not only about his approach to this study, but also about his values and his perception of his own strengths. The questions he wanted to pursue, rather than toys and games, became the focus of his next project. Reuben's processfolio gave the teacher and Reuben far more information about Reuben as a learner than would a portfolio containing only a finished product.

as the principal or teachers from another school, the child should be given the opportunity to explain portfolio content either in writing or orally.

All portfolio items should also be dated. If the portfolio item reflects a group process, this should be noted. Portfolios might include the following samples of student work (taken in part from Stenmark 1989, pp. 8, 9):

1. written descriptions of the results of investigations
2. pictures, drawings, charts, graphs, diagrams, and statistical studies
3. extended analyses of problem-solving

4. responses to specific questions
5. group reports
6. photographs of finished projects
7. audio, video, and computer-generated examples of student work
8. copies of awards and prizes
9. creative writing
10. original extensions of classroom work, such as musical composition, dance, drama

The advantages of portfolios are clearly documented by the following:

1. evidence of performance beyond factual knowledge gained
2. assessment records that reflect the emphasis of authentic learning
3. a permanent and long-term record of student progress
4. a clear and understandable picture of the assessment process
5. opportunities for improved student self-image as the result of showing accomplishments rather than deficiencies
6. a recognition of different learning styles
7. making assessment less culturally dependent and less biased
8. an active role for students in assessing and selecting their work

Interviews
One of the best ways of learning about a child is by talking with that child, asking both specific and open-ended questions that provide information to both teacher and child about the child's learning. The interview provides information about the child's thinking rather than the products of that thinking. Many children are able to produce correct answers but have little or no understanding of what these answers really mean or even if the answers are actually correct.

Assessment questions should be focused. The teacher needs to be clear on the direction of the interview so that he or she can follow a line of questioning that will yield the desired information. It is important for the teacher to allow enough time for a child to process and respond to a question. The teacher can ask a child to elaborate on a response or to demonstrate a thinking process.

It is helpful for the teacher to prepare a list of possible questions ahead of time, depending on the focus of the interview. However, the teacher needs to be flexible about changing the direction of the questioning if the child's responses indicate this need. The teacher also must provide a comfortable and nonthreatening atmosphere for the interview. A child should not be made to feel that he or she is being "tested" or that a "right answer" is required. The teacher should also apprise the child of the reason for the interview and that he or she will be taking notes in order to remember the important points. If the teacher and child agree, video- or audiotaping is helpful as it allows teacher and child to interact without the distraction of note-taking.

Some major advantages of the interview process are: (1) the opportunity for the teacher to attend solely to an individual child, providing the child with a sense of personal worth, (2) obtaining information about the child's feelings, fears, and perceptions of successes, which can be helpful in future planning, and (3) gaining an understanding of the child's thought processes as well as level of skills.

Some examples of interview questions are:

1. How would you describe this problem?
2. Can you explain that in your own words?
3. Where can you find the information you need?
4. Why do you think that didn't work?
5. How do you feel about your participation in your group?
6. What do you like best about your story?
7. What gave you the most problem in deciding how to approach this research?
8. How could you have solved that conflict with the others at your table so that you didn't go away mad?
9. Can you demonstrate with some math manipulatives how you got that answer?
10. Do you have a "system," strategy, or plan for solving this problem?

Interviews take time. Teachers can set aside a specific time for each child weekly or biweekly. This time can be as limited as five minutes or as extensive as thirty minutes depending on the maturity level of the child and the kind of information the teacher wants to obtain. It is important that the teacher plan interview time so that other members of the class are actively engaged in projects that do not require constant supervision. Children can be helped to respect each other's interview time.

Student Self-Assessment

Processfolios, portfolios, and interviews all provide opportunity for student self-assessment. Children also can be helped to assess their progress and products by the use of questionnaires at the end of a particular learning experience, or by having children specifically write about what they have just learned or experienced. Helping children to become reflective learners contributes to the metacognitive process in an important way. In addition, the reflective learner is more apt to really integrate information and generalize from a specific situation to others with similar components. Examples of questions that children can be asked following a learning activity are:

1. Describe what you learned from this activity.
2. How does this relate to what you have learned before?
3. What questions do you have now?

4. What don't you understand about this activity?
5. What is your plan for getting the additional information you need for a better understanding?
6. What contribution did you make to your group?
7. What did you feel best about with this activity?
8. What would you change if you were to do this activity again?

Students can provide feedback for each other that contributes to the self-assessment process. Viewing other student work can help an individual child develop standards for his or her own growth and assessment. The teacher should help children learn how to give each other constructive, informative feedback. Through this process, children learn to look at their work critically, but from the standpoint of using this information as the basis for improvement. The process of self-assessment may be new for many children. Children need many opportunities in many different situations to engage in the self-assessment process. Teachers can encourage self-assessment by honoring what children say about their own learning and making certain that there is no "right" or "wrong" approach or answer. If the classroom supports risk-taking and multiple perspectives on learning, then self-assessment is a natural part of the process. The teacher also can be a model for reflective practice and for self-assessment by sharing with the children his or her feelings and observations about how the activity was carried out, and by using the same kinds of questions and reflective journals in his or her assessment of his or her own practice.

Audio- and Videotapes

As mentioned previously, audio- and videotapes are an effective means of collecting interview data. In addition, they are a valuable tool for recording a group's process. For example, tape-recording a cooperative learning activity can provide the teacher with insight into such things as group decision-making, leadership patterns, and the group's methods for resolving conflicts. Videotapes provide a history of how an individual child or a group demonstrated an understanding of a concept or an activity. Videotapes also provide opportunity for children to review their own presentations for analysis and editing. Teachers can use videotapes as well as audiotapes for self-assessment, particularly in terms of their interactions with children. Videotapes provide a wealth of information as to the nonverbal behavior of the teacher.

Checklists

Checklists are simple ways of collecting information when the teacher wants to know if a child can do a particular task or demonstrate a particular skill. Checklists can be placed in different workspaces around the room. Children and teachers both can use a checklist. Some examples of checklists follow:

Student's Name _____

TECHNIQUES
  Selects appropriate book
  Reads at comfortable rate
  Appears relaxed
  Reads for information
  Reads for pleasure
MECHANICS
  Sight vocabulary
  Decoding
  Context clues
  Self-corrects
COMPREHENSION
  Retells story
  Interprets pictures
  States main idea
  Predicts
  Relates to similar experiences
  Fact or fiction
  Interprets character's feelings

Comments: _____
_____
_____

WRITING QUALITY
  Self-selects topics
  Builds vocabulary
  Expands sentences
  Experiments with styles
    Fact, Fiction, Drama
  Revises
  Meaningful text
MECHANICS
  Handwriting
  Periods & Capitals
  ? and !
  " " and .
  Spelling

Comments: _____
_____
_____

FIGURE 5-1   Reading–Writing Checklist

Source: Marge Jones

Student's Name _____

Introduced
Understood
Mastered

	Introduced	Understood	Mastered	
NUMBER SENSE				
Patterns				
Sorting				
Classifying				
Sequencing				
Predicting				
Estimating				
Number recognition				
Part-whole (fractions)				
Collecting & analyzing data				
Graphing				
Place value				
Problem solving				
MEASUREMENT				
Linear				
Weight				
Volume				
Time				
Money				
COMPUTATION				
+ Process				
+ Facts				
– Process				
– Facts				
+ – Relationship				
× Process				
× Facts				
– Process				
– Facts				
× – Relationship				
Calculator equations				

Comments: _____
_____
_____
_____
_____
_____
_____
_____

FIGURE 5-2 Math Checklist

Source: Marge Jones

Frequency Charts

Frequency charts answer the question "how often?" If a teacher wants to know how many times a particular child leaves his or her workspace during a set period of time, the teacher would use a frequency chart. Time frames are determined by a set period of observation. Frequency charts also provide information as to problem times for a child. To take a previous example, a child may be particularly disruptive right before lunch and at no other time

Distracting Behaviors
1. Initiates arguments
2. Initiates irrelevant conversations
3. Asks other children to complete work
4. Tosses manipulatives

Child's Name _____
(Use code for confidentiality)

A.M.		P.M.	
9:00 to 9:30	2 2 3 3 2 2 3	12:30 to 12:45	
9:30 to 9:45	2 2 2	12:45 to 1:00	
9:45 to 10:00		1:00 to 2:00	
10:00 to 10:15	1 4 2 2 1 1 4 2 1 1 3	2:00 to 3:00	
10:15 to 10:30	2 2 1 2 1 1 4 4	3:00 to 3:15	
10:30 to 10:45	1 1 4 1 2 2 4	3:15 to 3:45	
10:45 to 11:00	1 1 4 3 3 1 2 2 4 2	3:45 to 4:00	
11:00 to 11:15		4:00 to 4:15	
11:15 to 11:30		4:15 to 4:30	
11:30 to 11:45		4:30 to 4:45	
11:45 to 12:00		4:45 to 5:00	
12:00 to 12:15			
12:15 to 12:30			

Comments:

FIGURE 5-3 Frequency Chart

during the day. Working backwards, the teacher may discover that this child may not have had an adequate breakfast, and that the disruptive behavior could be altered by a midmorning snack. It is important for the teacher to define what, exactly, he or she plans to chart. If a teacher is using a term such as *distracting behavior,* he or she should specify exactly what that means, for example, the child is initiating an argument with a peer, initiating conversation not relevant to the task, asking another child to complete his or her portion of the work assignment, or tossing manipulatives around.

The frequency chart in figure 5-3 on page 111, for example, would provide the teacher with important information about Suzanne. First, the teacher would note that the majority of the distracting behavior occurs when Suzanne is working on the group project, which is from 10:00 to 11:00. The amount of time Suzanne tosses manipulatives around or initiates arguments with a peer is clearly high. During other time periods, Suzanne's distracting behavior is limited to asking the teacher questions unrelated to the task or asking another child to complete her work. The teacher notes that Suzanne's behavior during group time not only keeps her but also her classmates from completing the project. Prior to collecting the information on the frequency chart, the teacher assumed that Suzanne was just basically a troublemaker. Now the teacher wonders, given all the information from the chart, whether Suzanne has the background knowledge necessary to contribute to the group's project and for individual activities, or whether she might feel unable to do her work without teacher or peer assistance. In addition, the teacher questions whether Suzanne might need some help in developing group process skills. Using the frequency chart helped the teacher make a more accurate diagnosis of Suzanne's problem behavior: without this information, the teacher might have continued to view Suzanne as "just a behavior problem." It is important for the teacher to gather information using a frequency chart over a period of time to determine a pattern before drawing any inferences. Certain behaviors are more salient to a teacher than others. If a behavior is particularly annoying, this behavior will feel like it is happening all the time. Frequency charts help to put behavior in perspective.

Who-to-Whom Charts

Who-to-whom charts are easy ways to determine leadership patterns in a group, as well as to better understand peer group relationships. The teacher indicates the space occupied by each child in the group and then documents who initiates the conversation, to whom it is directed, and if there is a response. This is done over a given period of time, say fifteen minutes.

The teacher, from looking at this who-to-whom chart at the top of page 113, can now better plan to help all the children become more effective members of this group. The teacher has had particular concerns about J, since he always seems so unhappy about not being part of this group. By

---

Who-to-Whom Chart

Observations from chart: Oct. 14, 1992
Observations of peer interaction with particular focus on *K*.

B is the leader of this group. *S*, *G*, and *K* are all part of *B*'s group. *K* has the least status. *J* would like to be in this group but does not recognize that *B* is the leader and that *K* has less status than *S* or *G*. *B* would like *M* to become part of the group but *M* seems more interested in *P* from another group.

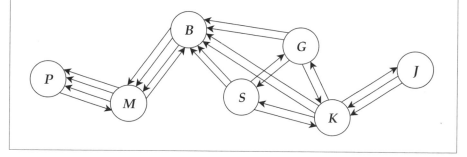

---

helping *J* understand that *B* is the leader and how best to approach *B* and other high status group members, she can assist *J* in developing social skills that will promote his acceptance. In addition, knowing that *B* is the leader will help the teacher focus on the skills *B* needs to develop to be a more responsible leader. Without the documented evidence, it would be easy to assume that *J* is initiating contact with his group and being rejected, when, in reality, he is initiating contact with the group member who has little status and little ability to bring him into the group. In addition, *B* might not be recognized clearly as the leader of the group. If a teacher wants a group to accept a child not presently a member of that group, or to change the dynamics of how that group operates, it is important that the teacher work with rather than against the natural leader of the group.

Running Records

A running record is a continuous flow of observations that is made as a teacher observes a child or group of children over a specified length of time. The teacher must be careful not to include any reactions or inferences in these observations. When the observations are completed, they are analyzed for patterns.

The information the teacher gained from the record on page 114 will direct him to focus more closely on how *K* perceives himself as a learner. *K*, throughout this record, makes a number of comments that indicate he has real questions about his capability, not just to do puzzles, but to do school

---

Running Record

Child's name: K
Date: Oct. 4, 1992
Setting: Classroom
Beginning record: 9 am
End of record: 9:20 am

J and *K* are working together on a puzzle. *J:* "I'm mad at *B*." *K:* "So am I." *J:* "*B* said I couldn't play with him and his sister if my mom took us to visit this weekend." *K:* "*B*'s mean." *J:* "You're not doing this puzzle right." *K:* "I guess I don't know how to do puzzles." *J:* "You can't do math either." *K:* "I'm not very smart am I?" *J:* "Stop putting the pieces in the wrong place!" *K:* "I don't know how to do puzzles." ect.

---

work in general. The running record, because it is a continuous script, allows the teacher to have many examples in a short period of time to support a child's thinking and behavioral patterns.

Anecdotal Records

Anecdotal records act as a "snapshot" of an event. The teacher uses language to describe the event as vividly as possible, including what the child said, and how he or she said it, complete with nonverbal gestures. The record also includes what the child did, and what happened in response. The record continues until the particular event is complete. The more the teacher can "paint a picture" with words, the more meaningful the anecdote. Anecdotal records, as well as all records, should state the date, time of day, and activity.

The teacher collected a number of these anecdotal records before analyzing them for patterns. All the anecdotals that dealt with journal writing were similar. It appeared that when *S* felt that he had to state what he was

---

Anecdotal Record

Child's name: S
Setting: Classroom
Date: Oct. 5, 1992
Activity: Journal writing
Time: 11:00 am

S slowly picked his journal out of the box and plopped it down on the table. His fists were clenched at his side, and his eyes were downcast. One of the other children asked *S* what he was going to write about in his journal. *S* responded in a loud voice that he did not know and he did not care. He stared at the journal cover for about a minute, then got up quickly and found a corner where he could be alone. He then began writing with concentration, and did not stop for almost ten minutes. When he completed his journal he smiled and put it back in the storage box.

---

going to write about prior to writing he became annoyed and defensive. When he was able to find a place away from the other children, he approached his journal with enthusiasm. The teacher made certain that there was no pressure put on *S* to discuss his journal entries with other members of the class. In addition, he made certain that there was always a personal space for *S* to use while journal writing. Without these records, the teacher might not have been as supportive. He may have taken the position that *S* did not want or like to make journal entries when in fact this was one of his favorite activities. What *S* did not like was the feeling that he needed to share his personal thoughts with others.

Teacher Self-Evaluation

Teachers can use a variety of methods for self-evaluation. As for children, a journal is an excellent way for a teacher to examine his or her own processes and evolution as a professional. A journal should not be objective: it is a place for the teacher to express feelings, ideas, concerns, and frustrations without judgment. Journal entries should be dated and periodically reviewed. From reading past entries, the teacher can observe patterns of behavior, reactions to certain children, satisfaction or frustration with particular approaches, and methodologies.

Journal Entries

February: I have not been pleased with journal writing. I am getting minmal writing and there seems to be a lack of interest in writing.

I give the kids a topic (usually dealing with social/peer problems) to write about; afterward we would sit in circle and discuss what they wrote. We have some great discussions, but little writing, and writing is my emphasis.

February: I have been giving some thought to journal time. A journal should be a diary of one's thoughts and a record of important events.

February: I have decided to try combining sharing time with journal writing. Everyone (including myself) will write about something they would like to share with the class; however, reading journal entries will be voluntary.

February: I have been disturbed/unsatisfied with my role as teacher or coach. I give directions and corrections, praise and critique, I encourage and give reminders, but in all these situations I am still looked to for approval and final evaluation of projects. I want the kids to also evaluate their projects. Were they happy with the project and why, or were they dissatisfied and why.

March: I am thrilled with what's been happening during journal time. I have had to increase the time we spend on writing in our journals. Journal writing has turned into a time to record events, jokes, personal thoughts, and a variety of other topics. Most of the kids read their entries. We still discuss social/peer problems, because someone usually writes about a problem.

I have decided to keep their journals for the three years they are with me. I think they will enyoy reading them at the end of three years.

March: I added another feature to journal writing, I've asked the kids to write to me on Fridays. Of course, I write back. At first most of the Friday entries were personal, i. e. questions about my favorite color, sport, hobby, or my age and how long I have been married, etc. Lately some of the children are writing about peer problems, what they have liked or disliked about topics we have studied, and ideas about future themes.

Their journals have turned into a valuable means of recording and communicating their thoughts. Journal writing now has a purpose for them and it is meeting my expectations.

March: I have instituted some changes during activity time. When they finish their projects they evaluate their work. They give themselves an excellent, okay, or poor, and tell me why.

This system is working well. Sometimes a child gives him/herself an excellent, even though little information was given. But he/she spent lots of time researching and there just wasn't much information available. They are beginning to see areas they could have done better on or worked harder on. I'm finding the kids are very honest about their evaluations.

March: The kids are discovering areas they need to improve on during project/activity time. I'm having to give fewer suggestions.

March: The last two themes we have studied I've asked the kids to write an essay (or dictate) what they know about the subject before we start the theme. At the end of the theme they write another essay on what they have learned about the subject.

After the before and after essays I am amazed at the amount of information they picked up. I am often surprised at areas of interest within the theme.

The essays have given the kids and me better feedback than the tests I had given on earlier themes.

March: Recently I started participating in more activities with the kids. I write journal entries and share them, I participate in P.E., I write a weekly article for our classroom paper, and I do a part of our holiday bulletin board.

Has my participation made an impact on their learning? I keep asking myself this question. Through my participation, I am constantly modeling (no lecturing) what to do. I also told them I am doing these activities because I want to join in on the fun. They see my interest and enthusiasm and pick up on it. I feel my participation sparks their interest.

March: I have decided to expand my "projects". I am going to include publishing, science experiments, and some research reports. Not only will I continue to demonstrate, but this will be a way I can fill in gaps on topics I feel important.

April: Some of the kids have written to me about their dissatisfaction with the themes we have covered this year. Even though they picked the topics and we voted on them at the beginning of the year, we could only cover the top seven.

April: I have been giving some thought to how I could change activity (theme) time to suit everyone. I think next year I will let each child pick his/her own theme to investigate. I will use a contract system under each theme they choose to help them with the planning. Our weekly trips to the library will involve their checking out books and films for information.

Judy Tyson

Audio- and videotapes provide information about teacher/child interactions, teacher verbal and nonverbal behavior, and management techniques. It is helpful to have a trusted colleague review video- and audiotapes for a less subjective evaluation. Review of other teachers' tapes can help sharpen observations, providing more detailed feedback to the teacher. In addition, it provides opportunities for teachers to develop standards and criteria for performance. Creating these trust relationships provides teachers with a forum for discussing their classroom practices and receiving ongoing feedback.

Sample questions for a tape analysis:

1. Describe your tone of voice. Does your tone vary in expression? Does it convey acceptance or impatience? Would you feel comfortable taking risks as a learner given your tone of voice?

2. What is the nature of your verbalization? Do you ask many questions? What kind of questions do you tend to ask most? Do you need to expand any one type of questioning (factual, evaluative, interpretive, extending, or eliciting)? Are your questions those that would assist children to problem-solve? Do you ask questions that would help children understand their thinking about a problem? Do you use a variety of questions to help children predict and estimate? Do you ask questions that help children relate what they are doing to past experiences and real-life problems?

3. How responsive are you to what children are saying? Are you *really* listening? How do you know? Are you more responsive to certain children than to others?

4. How often do you acknowledge children ? What is the nature of this acknowledgement?

5. How do you provide feedback to children regarding their performance? Do you tend to make global statements such as "good job," or do you tend to be more specific?

Student Evaluation of Classroom

All children should have opportunities to give feedback to the teacher about all aspects of life in the classroom. Children can be helped to understand how to give feedback constructively. Children can be encouraged to complete sentences designed to elicit their ideas and feelings about learning and the environment. Statements and questions may include:

I liked the way _____

I did not like _____

I found _____ to be particularly difficult because _____

I liked working with my group because _____

I did not like working with my group because _____

Other children were _____

The teacher was _____

The teacher could have helped me more by _____

Younger children can do pictorial representations of how they feel about the class, specific lessons, and the teacher. They also can talk into a tape recorder for later review by the teacher. Group problem-solving sessions are a positive technique for both older and younger children. The teacher or the children can present the problem for discussion. The teacher and the children should establish ground rules for discussion in advance to ensure that no child is "picked on," and that the focus is kept on constructive solutions.

Things to Remember

In the integrated classroom, children are busy, active, and involved. There are many opportunities for the teacher to observe and listen. Children reveal important information about themselves when the teacher least expects it to happen. Teachers should always be alert to children's actions and reactions and be ready to make notes, in whatever abbreviated form, to be analyzed at a later time. Having pencils and paper or file cards, checklists, frequency charts, who-to-whom charts, and tape recorders ready at all times is important. The teacher who organizes data collection tools in advance, and carries a small pad or file cards and a pencil at all times when interacting with children, is more likely to compile information in a meaningful and systematic way. If the teacher takes the time to summarize data on a regular basis, it will be easy to utilize this information in planning and evaluating classroom activity both for the individual child and the group. A major concern when collecting data is confidentiality. Children have as much right as adults to their privacy. Observations should be coded with numbers or letters so that no one but the teacher can know who the data concerns. Summary records and interpretations of data should be kept in locked files. Files can be made available to parents, and under certain circumstances, the courts. Any information that becomes part of a student's record must be carefully documented, and screened for subjectivity and bias.

Suggested Activities

1. Observe a group of children working cooperatively on a task. Write down your observations in a journal, and then use your notes as the basis for describing each child's developmental level, and what behaviors are specific indicators of these levels. Once you have determined the developmental levels, evaluate the appropriateness of the activity for all those taking part.

2. With another teacher, observe a group of children during a work period. Keep a running record of what you observe. Compare your record with that

of the other teacher. Make a list of the differences in your observations. See if you can determine what aspects of the children's activity *you* tend to focus on and what aspects the other teacher tends to focus on. How do these tendencies influence your objectivity?

3. Tape-record a group of children interacting in a social setting. Using a who-to-whom chart, plot the directions of the interactions, and write a summary that would include such things as: which child received the most verbalizations, which children appeared to be high status members of the group, was there any child who made an attempt to be recognized that was discounted, and why was it discounted. Develop a plan to assist any child who is being unsuccessful in the group.

4. Write a series of anecdotal records on a particular child. Use as many different words as possible to describe the child's actions and words. Give these records to another teacher who does not know this child. Protect confidentiality by removing the child's name from these records first. Ask the other teacher to tell you about this child. If you have used a wide variety of descriptive words, the other teacher should be able to tell you about the child in so much detail that you would think the teacher actually knew the child.

5. Tape-record your interactions with a group of children. Using the tape analysis questions, analyze your tape. When you have completed your analysis, develop a plan for change. Make sure that you include an explanation of the reasons for the various components of this plan. Tape-record again in one month, and determine how you are doing with your plan. Continue to record and analyze until you feel you have accomplished the initial goals.

6. Keep a processfolio on the development of your observational skills. Take the time to review this processfolio on a regular basis to determine if the whole idea of assessment is becoming more natural and more a part of your daily interactions with children. Some things that might go in your processfolio could include: initial notes and recordings, reactions and analyses, changes in how you think about a child over time, changes in how you decide to approach a particular observation of children or of yourself, specific assessment tools that you use and your reactions to them, a documentation of how interview questions have changed over time to better elicit desired information, and the process or processes that you develop for assessment, planning, and evaluation.

7. Keep a portfolio of your best observations, examples of children's work that you have used for assessment or planning purposes, examples of these plans and how they relate to your observations, any written summaries of readings on the topic of assessment or copies of the articles themselves, video- or audiotapes that demonstrate your particular strengths, samples of interviews with children that provided information that was really useful, and student assessments of classroom and teacher.

References

Gardner, Howard. (1993). *Multiple Intelligences: The Theory in Practice.* New York: Basic Books.

Goodman, Yetta. (1978). *Kid-watching: An Alternative to Testing.* National Elementary Principal. 57 (4), 41–45.

Stenmark, Jean Kerr. (1989). *Assessment Alternatives in Mathematics.* California: Mathematics Council.

6

Planning for Meaningful Learning

In schools, therefore, let the students learn to write by writing, to talk by talking, to sing by singing, and to reason by reasoning. In this way schools will become workshops humming with work, and students whose efforts prove successful will experience the truth of the proverb "We give form to ourselves and to the materials at the same time." (John Amos Comenius in Yeomans, 1969, p. 27)

A Window into Two Classrooms

Classroom 1: An Integrated Group

The following quotation from *Learning and Loving It* best describes what we have defined as an integrated classroom where meaningful learning occurs in a learner-supportive way:

> *There are piles of books, posters and diagrams. There are files, newspaper clippings, fishermen's journals and what have you to aid the children in their inquiry . . . Fishing tackle is in the middle of the room and a lobster trap entices one from under an array of crayons and colored pencils. The message is clear: this is a* learning-investigating *(emphasis ours) environment. Please talk, exchange ideas, voice your opinions. Please don't be quiet! The learners are center stage. This is their environment. They created it and roam around in it, with a couple of adults "standing by." These are their teachers or learning facilitators . . .*
>
> *Learning is a process here, not an end product delivered to the children by a lecturing teacher in the front of the room. Absent are the traditional perimeters of the classroom. There are no rows of anonymous desks, but rather*

scattered around the room are round and square tables where groups of chil-
dren . . . work. Everyone is working on something whether it be writing a
thank-you letter to someone who showed them slides of "fishing in developed
and underdeveloped countries" or finishing research on a given topic.

What the teachers do is prompt, advise, initiate the discussions which
lead to new ideas and stimulate heated debate. They organize the great wealth
of resource materials which replace the traditional classroom texts . . . they are
there not to force their particular points of view on the children, but rather to
point out to them the wealth of knowledge, the many different points of view
out there from which they must choose—in school, as well as in life in gener-
al. (Christine Cudmore-Kear in Gamberg, et al., 1988, p. 9)

The teacher in this classroom plays many roles: prompter, advisor, ini-
tiator, stimulator, observer, coach, resource, planner and organizer, facilitator, evaluator, curriculum developer, as well as "teacher" in the traditional
sense when necessary. The teacher's role is ever-changing, as it is dictated
by the needs of the children.

Classroom 2: A Traditional Setting

The desks are neatly lined up in rows facing the front of the room. The
teacher has planned the day in terms of subject disciplines and time allot-
ments. Using the texts adopted by the district, he plans for the isolated
lessons which he will teach at given times during the day. Even though it is
understood that any good teacher goes beyond what is designated in the
textbook, constraints are still there, either overtly or covertly. Basically, the
traditional teacher thinks in terms of "delivering" lessons on a particular
subject, in a whole-group presentation, at a predetermined time. Most often
the lesson is stopped at the end of the time frame, regardless of whether
children need or want more time. The teacher's role is singular: plan one lesson for each discipline. The lesson usually takes the form of lecture/expla-
nation followed by workbook pages, all to be completed within a given time
slot. Children who do not finish are sometimes kept in from recess or given
the work to do as homework—a clear message that they are not as quick or
as capable as some of their peers. If there is a "second role" for the teacher,
it is that of disciplinarian, keeping order and quiet.

Teaching in this setting proceeds from the philosophy of the need for
children to learn a predetermined body of knowledge within a school year.
This predetermined body of knowledge is usually directed by the state or
district guidelines, and almost always by a textbook, none of which are
always sensitive to developmental issues or individual children's needs. It
is presumed to be "more efficient" to teach all children the same thing at the
same time, but the question must be raised: "more efficient" for whom?

The Roles of the Teacher: An Expansion of Terms

The role of the teacher is never more critical than in an integrated classroom; in actuality, the teacher in this setting has many roles, not just a single role. No matter how perfect the environment in terms of architecture and arranged or provisioned space, it is the teacher who is the most important factor in making the educational experience a positive, growing one for each child. In the traditional setting, the teacher's role is relatively static. The teacher implements the predetermined curriculum that is most likely text-book driven. Curriculum content and method of delivery usually do not vary in accordance with children's developmental changes, background, and learning/working style. The lesson, whatever it may be, is delivered to the whole class at the same time in the same way.

In the integrated setting, the teacher's role is never static; it changes constantly with each child, small groups of children, and even the entire class. Sometimes the teacher offers direct instruction, while at other times, his or her role is facilitator of small group processes. At still other times, the teacher's role may be co-investigator with children. The role of the teacher is one of extensive personal interactions as he or she models, learns, coaches, and guides. Curriculum evolves, depending upon the children's changing interests and needs, but it is always tied to a predetermined set of goals or outcomes decided by the teacher, reflecting state/district goals as well as those of the parents. The process of teaching in an integrated setting is one of arranging learning experiences and possibilities for expanding and refining the concept development and skills of the children in that classroom. A school in the Santa Fe, New Mexico, district arranges for a day when parents and children meet individually with teachers to jointly set goals for the children's year, thus ensuring that both academic and social needs are addressed from three important perspectives.

Teacher Beliefs

First and most importantly, the integrated teacher must hold a firm belief in the *ability* and *desire* of the child to learn, with proper guidance and a minimum of interference from a knowledgeable adult. Regardless of socioeconomic background, ethnic ties, or language, all children come to school with experiences in the real world on which learning can be built or expanded, becoming a major part of curriculum content.

> *To begin with, the child of 5, 6, or 7 is in many ways an extremely competent individual. Not only can she use skillfully a raft of symbol forms, but she has evolved a galaxy of robust theories that prove quite serviceable for most pur-*

poses and can even be extended in a generative fashion to provide cogent
accounts of unfamiliar materials or processes. (Gardner, 1991, p. 110)

Children learn to talk without direct teaching, and to negotiate their social environment with different degrees of finesse and success. Children's learning and growth develop over *spans* of time, not in neatly quantified discrete units. For example, children are considered normal if they learn to walk somewhere between nine and fourteen months. Acquiring literacy and numeracy over a span of years should be considered no less normal. Children do not grow, develop, and acquire skills at exactly the same time and in the same way. It cannot be emphasized enough that teachers need to understand developmental levels: physical, social–emotional, and cognitive including brain development and function. Being knowledgeable and comfortable with child development theory makes decision making for all aspects of curriculum easier and more efficient.

Teacher as Co-Investigator

The teacher of the twenty-first century must be a model as an ongoing learner. Children must see teachers engaged in the daily use of literacy and numeracy, problem solving, and the creative process. The teacher is a guide, providing children with appropriate activities in the right sequence to ensure the understanding of needed concepts. The teacher is a resource person who not only provides necessary materials but knows where and to whom to send children for further inquiry and study. The teacher as coach knows when to urge a child on, when to back off and not interfere with the thought processes, and when to introduce some "conflict" that will ensure disequilibrium, accommodation, and assimilation. Rather than being the dispenser of knowledge and the holder of vast stores of facts and figures to give away, the teacher becomes part of the learning process along with the children. It is expected that a well-prepared teacher will have a broad understanding of the content that is going to be investigated, but it is unrealistic to expect that a teacher will have expert knowledge of every subject area. When children have more responsibility in initiating the content of learning, the teacher must give up the idea of being a storehouse of data. Clearly it is not necessary to be a mechanical engineer to orchestrate a theme study on systems. In this instance, the teacher can learn more about systems and what they do along with the children. What is crucial for the teacher is knowing where to get resources and how to provision for hands-on experiences for children, as well as providing opportunities for research and reading.

Being a catalyst or co-investigator in the learning process does not mean that the teacher never teaches directly; that is, plans and delivers a directed lesson on some specific concept, topic, or skill. An integrated classroom is not an abdication of responsibility as teacher in the traditional sense. Children, at times, require directed lessons. Forms of instruction vary according to what is appropriate for a child or a group of children at any given time. Directed lessons in an integrated environment serve to give children a needed boost up the cognitive ladder. The most appropriate time for this boost is when there is a demonstrated need. Children give out strong messages, sometimes overtly and sometimes covertly, telling the teacher what is needed at any particular time. The teacher's role, then, is to be alert to those signals and to act upon them. The integrated classroom strongly supports the concept of the subordination of teaching to learning.

Kid-Watcher and Listener

For teachers to be alert and responsive to children's changing needs, they must acquire the ability to be good "kid-watchers" (Goodman, Y., 1978). In the traditional classroom, where the teacher is required to "deliver" lessons, learning the skills of kid-watching is almost an impossibility. The teacher's focus is, out of necessity, on the delivery of content and student response. Often, the format of instruction is brief question and answer. Whole-class instruction often limits the time available to the teacher to probe and pursue an idea, concept, or direction which would provide information as to what a child knows, and more importantly, what he or she is in the process of knowing. Being able to stand back, watch, and listen carefully while children interact with each other and materials provides the opportunity to gather the information necessary for further planning and evaluation as described in Chapter 5.

An integrated classroom provides the time necessary to follow through with a child, to lead the child into that critical zone of proximal development so that the teacher can note what the child can do with assistance as opposed to what he or she can do entirely on his or her own. This information promotes teacher decision making that speaks to what the child needs to move on to the next level of cognitive understanding.

Maria Marolda, mathematics specialist at the Learning Disabilities Clinic of Boston Children's Hospital, states that children frequently know their own difficulties, and if listened to carefully and watched mindfully, they will assist the adult in helping them. Marolda points out that careful watching of children in mathematics using manipulative materials can help a teacher determine the strengths and deficits in the child's brain organization. Using these cues and clues makes it infinitely easier to plan both short and long term for that child's learning, in mathematics and in other areas as well. A teacher observing two children doing the same task can learn a child's preferred choice of materials and strategies for problem solving.

For example, a child is given the basic arithmatic problem of 14 minus 5. Strategy one: Does the child choose chips to use as counters (a discrete model for number)? Strategy two: Does the child use cuisenaire rods (a continuous or measurement model for number)? Strategy three: Does the child count orally backwards from 14 ("13-12-11-10-9: the answer is 9")? Strategy four: Does the child count up orally on his fingers from 5 ("6-7-8-9-10-11-12-13-14: the answer is 9")? This requires that the child keep track of not only the "count sequence," but also of the quantity of the count.

Here are four vastly different approaches to the same problem. The child counting backwards from 14 is either thinking on a number line, whether or not this model is in his or her head or in front of him or her, or is physically removing five chips from a pile of fourteen. The child who is counting up from 5 either understands that subtraction and addition are clearly related, or is using rods to model the concept "what do I add to 5 to get to 14?" The problem for the teacher, then, is to help the child to use his or her strengths to approach whatever new problems and concepts he or she confronts, *and* to work with the child to increase his or her understanding and abilities to use other approaches and strategies. One of the major advantages in the use of manipulative materials in the classroom is the insight they provide into the thinking processes of the child. If the classroom is not arranged to allow the children maximum time for their own investigations and explorations, there is little time for the teacher to kid-watch or kid-listen.

Teacher Decisions: Goals and Objectives of Instruction

Although teachers are required to make instantaneous decisions throughout the day, it is very important to have both long- and short-term goals and objectives for the entire group and for individual children. In Chapter 5, assessment was discussed in terms of understanding children and as a tool for the planning of appropriate instruction. The first questions that a teacher must ask when planning goals and objectives for meaningful learning include: What should happen in this classroom? What behaviors of children should be encouraged? What behaviors of children should be discouraged? And, what should children learn and how should they learn this? The following goal-setting model illustrates planning that spans four basic areas as shown at the top of page 127.

The decisions the teacher needs to make both long and short term are based on:

1. choices rooted in an understanding of theory.
2. comfort with various methods of teaching.
3. knowledge, understanding, and acceptance of how children learn best.

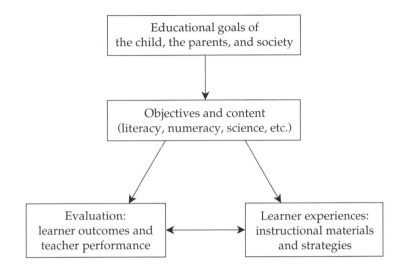

4. understanding the time constraints of the work environment as well as the constraints placed upon the teacher by the administration.
5. materials availability.
6. the teacher's own philosophical beliefs about active versus passive learners.

An Example of Decisions in a Multi-Age Classroom

Cooperative Learning Groups
In order to facilitate learning at different levels, to encourage the multi-ages to work together, and to encourage immediate use of learned information, I decided to set up cooperative learning groups using Spencer Kagan's models. Each group of four consisted of one high, one low, and two average achieving students. Age was not a determining factor. I felt I needed to place students in situations in which they would be forced to assume a variety of roles, or else (I feared) many of the younger students would fall into less active roles with the older students.

Use of graphic organizers to teach skilled decision making
El Dorado asks students to provide evidence for their opinions. Important in this is the ability to consider options, consequences, and importance of those consequences in a given situation. Too often educators assume that students know how to make decisions without giving them the tools to do so.

(continued)

(continued)

Use of Future Problem Solving (FPS) in the classroom with all students

Leaders in the workplace are telling educators that an essential skill for the twenty-first century will be the ability to collaborate in solving problems. FPS solicits ideas from all team members regardless of age or expertise. It teaches students to view a given situation from seventeen different perspectives. It is a nonjudgmental process in terms of what each team member brings, and therefore is excellent for a multi-age classroom.

Team building

Current brain research confirms that an effective learning environment must be free from anxiety and full of trust. Therefore I spent the better part of the first week of school engaging students in activities that encouraged trust and respect for one another. (The coming school year will again stress those activities, but will be more structured and run by a Ph.D. candidate.)

Grade level student participation with other grade level classes

My class was the only intermediate level multi-age classroom at El Dorado. I found that led to comparisons between our class and the other grade level classes by students and parents. I recognize that the emotional state of the students is equal in importance to academics. Therefore I allowed my sixth grade students to participate in a unit of study with other sixth grade classes. Following that, the fourth and fifth graders also requested that they be allowed to work with others of their grade levels. This was a big decision for me because to allow students to leave the classroom to work with grade level classes runs counter to the philosophy of multi-age classrooms. Yet until the majority of the school becomes multi-aged, students will continue to feel emotionally isolated from their peers.

Maya Festival

In an effort to empower my students and also to give them a chance to "show off" their knowledge after a study of the Mayas, I decided to have my class host a Maya Festival, in which students donned ceremonial masks they had made, wore Mayan costumes, wrote and produced skits about Mayan life, and planned and served a traditional Mayan feast. This was presented to the entire student body. It did indeed unite the class emotionally as well as providing a conduit for an exhibition of their knowledge of the Mayas.

Journaling

I chose to use the journal model called "Sources" from Interact. Each day students were to write a teacher-specified topic entry. For example, entry topics included autobiographical accounts, visualizations, dream recounts, major events in their lives, reactions to societal issues, conversations with oneself, one's body, etc. I read the journal entries unless a student requested that I not. I assessed writing ability (to an extent), thoughts, effort, knowledge, spelling, creativity, and other things specific to the assignment. Students kept their daily entries in a three-ring binder and were thus able to look back on their work.

Cooperative Learning Groups
I chose to use Spencer Kagan's cooperative learning structures and grouping strategies. I did not use team points because my goal was to help students define and monitor internal satisfaction with their performance rather than strive for external rewards. The grouping is vital and healthy for multi-aged students because it requires them to assume roles that might not be assumed given age and experiential differences.

Less is More
This concept is undoubtedly the most difficult and risky decision I made with my multi-age classroom. Several times throughout the year I gave an assignment which mushroomed beyond my expectations. As long as student interest remained, and as long as the tasks being performed were furthering answers to the essential question, I allowed activities to go on far longer than I had anticipated they would. This not only empowered students to seek knowledge, it also allowed me to provide instruction as it was needed for a task. True implementation of Less is More requires a willingness on the part of the teacher to let go of a certain amount of control, and a trust that students will learn what they need to learn for a given task.

Assessment
Students were usually aware of my expectations and of the tasks they would be required to perform. Toward the end of the school year I became more comfortable with student designs of assessment tasks. Because of the wide range of abilities, interests, and experiences of students in a multi-age classroom, I usually listed three or four performance tasks from which students were to select two. Students always knew that from any given assignment I was assessing a number of things. With this in mind students were forced to assume responsibility and to integrate skills. For example, they knew that it was their responsibility to spell correctly in all written work, be it math, social studies, a photo essay, etc.

I also chose to plan units beginning with the assessment—tasks that would allow the students to show what they know and are able to do. This helped all of us to focus on skills and knowledge that were necessary to the required performances, and it relieved much anxiety on the part of the students and placed more responsibility on them to ask for assistance on something they had not fully grasped.

Curriculum Development
The curriculum was based in part on a concept for the year: Change. Students were asked an essential question at the beginning of the year, and the question was referred to frequently by me until they were in the habit of referring to it themselves. The question was, "When does change become necessary?" With this concept in mind, assessment was designed to bring students closer to their own answer to the essential question. In literature we explored all kinds of

(continued)

(continued)

change, from writing style to character development to attitudinal changes within character. In math we looked at changes (especially in fractions). Social studies and sciences easily provided examples of change. Students periodically reread their journal entries to look for changes in their own lives.

So the curriculum was designed to not only help students answer the essential question, but also to practice all aspects of the required assessment. PLEASE NOTE: Although my curriculum differed significantly from traditional grade level curriculums, many of the themes I chose to present to students coincide with the school community's list of essential skills and body of knowledge. I simply have a greater latitude in terms of when material is covered, since I will have the same students for up to three years.

Spelling

I decided at the beginning of the school year NOT to give spelling tests, but rather to let students know that correct spelling was expected on every assignment. I taught dictionary, thesaurus, and computer skills to facilitate their spelling. When misspellings occurred in their work, those words were added to a growing vocabulary list, and various activities were assigned to encourage memorization, or at least more care in the future. I was pleased to note that misspellings were far less frequent from these students than from previous students who memorized words for a test and then frequently misspelled them in application.

Reading Program

The reading program I chose uses a compilation of strategies from Junior Great Books, adult book clubs, and a teacher-designed book contract. Since the Socratic method is frequently used in my classroom, students were taught how to design open-ended questions from their readings. Students selected novels to read from a list of about forty award-winning or popular books. There had to be three or more students reading the same book and designing questions. Book clubs met two to three times a week to discuss each others' questions and reactions to the book. When finished with each novel, students completed a book contract that required them to use each level of Bloom's Taxonomy.

This was the first time I had ever designed my own reading program. I knew that in a multi-age classroom with a three-year age span, reading abilities would vary widely. I hoped that student self-selection of reading material would meet individual needs as well as integrate the age groups, and I believe it did just that. I also chose this method in order to assess reading comprehension and ability to make inferences through questioning.

Math Instruction

Ironically, this was the area in which I felt the strongest, yet I found myself constantly revising my decisions. I based the math curriculum on the NCTM standards, and began the year spending approximately twenty percent of the time having students compute on paper. Almost daily the students were asked to use the date as the answer to an equation, the complexity of which I dictated for several students. I chose Marilyn Burns' books as my guide to activities which leant themselves to not only the NCTM standards, but also to partner or cooperative work. Because the class was multi-aged, I decided to extend many of the math activities by asking students to "teach" someone else the specific method(s) they had used in their own work. Since there is a ninety-five percent retention rate for learning when that knowledge is used immediately or taught, I frequently required that students teach each other.

I suppose I chose NOT to design the math program in any particular sequence, mostly because I couldn't see a purpose for doing so, and I didn't know how to prioritize the sequence either. I found that students were enthusiastic about the projects and activities using math, but I don't believe I gave them enough formal practice in computation, which they actually requested toward the end of the year.

At all times when appropriate, math vocabulary and concepts were integrated into the curriculum. I was completely pleased with that decision. However, the formal arithmetic component of my program was inadequate.

The Race Around the World
My school designed the social studies curriculum of knowledge by grade level: fourth would study regions of the U.S.; fifth, U.S. history; sixth, world history. I decided to follow that plan as well as I could while still adhering to the philosophy of multi-age classrooms. The Race Around the World is an integrated unit of study in which students assume the role of a magazine correspondent who travels to locations and writes informational articles for the magazine. I modified the original unit by formulating focus questions that would help students answer the essential question on "change," that would allow them to use their prior knowledge of U.S. regions, history, or the world, and that would emphasize the areas of culture, history, and geography as required by the state of New Mexico.

As the unit progressed, I realized that most of the students, regardless of age, did not know how to organize their articles, nor did they know how to synthesize information. They were looking for "the answer" to their focus question in one informational source. Therefore I began skills instruction with the entire class on use of reference materials, notetaking, outlining, and bibliographies. I also decided to break down the articles into smaller assignments due at the end of every or every other day.

I made one other major decision in this unit with multi-age students in mind: Students were required to write an article about a state within each of the six U.S. regions before they were permitted to "leave the country." I made this decision because all fourth graders at El Dorado were expected to be experts in knowledge of the regions, and I wanted to align our class with school consensus as much as possible. An unexpected bonus of this decision was a motivational factor for students to write more articles and to learn about the rest of the world.

(continued)

(continued)

Motivation
A little more than a year ago I read the work of Drs. Renate and Geoffrey Caine in ASCD's publication *Making Connections: Teaching and the Human Brain*. I was intrigued with studies that supported internal motivation over external motivation for retention of knowledge. Based on these studies I told students from day one that their work should be based on two criteria: that it be complete, and that they were proud of it. Students were then involved in defining what qualities in work should make one proud. I reminded them of those criteria frequently, and after a few months I found that several students seemed to have internalized them and began reminding members of their cooperative learning group about those criteria. I wanted students to develop their own internal yardsticks by which to measure their performance, and to move away from working for a grade or for someone else's standards.

Source: Bonnie Barnes, Teacher, El Dorado Elementary School, Santa Fe, New Mexico.

As the teacher grows in experience and continues to learn, decisions are thoughtfully pondered, frequently questioned, and sometimes changed, but always carefully executed and implemented. This is the key difference between a thoughtful, reflective teacher and a technician, one who delivers the prescribed lessons of another.

Opinions of teachers that can get in the way of thoughtful, reflective decision making are:

1. "I don't really remember much about Piaget and I don't have time to read."
2. "I'm not comfortable letting kids investigate on their own. What happens if they don't get what they need to know?"
3. "I know this isn't the way children learn best, but I'm going to do it anyway. I'm not spending every waking hour thinking, planning, and provisioning for children."
4. "If I don't end my lessons on time, I won't be able to cover the materials in the day's plans."
5. "I'm not going to try this. My principal won't let me."
6. "If the district won't provide the materials, I can't provide the instruction."
7. "I never thought much about my philosophical beliefs."

These kinds of opinions tend to block the teacher from thinking creatively and in new ways about the learning-teaching environment. Gardner (1993) states that his vision of the "individual-centered school" is neither utopian nor out of reach financially: it is belief in the concept and the will to make it happen that underscore such change.

For a professional new to the field or for one who is shifting from a more traditional approach to an integrated one, it is helpful to use the previously described goal-setting model as a way of encouraging thinking about a vastly different type of classroom environment that looks much more loosely structured. This planning process should free the teacher's thinking from preconceived ideas about the delivery of instruction and the learning process, allowing for a more holistic view of the educational experience and more developmentally appropriate decisions. As part of this planning process, the teacher should include theoretical constructs, the organization of the day, the availability of resources, learning processes, and outcomes. The teacher should then reflect on these as they relate to his or her belief system about how children learn and how teachers teach.

Working through the planning process in written form helps to clarify, for the teacher, where he or she is going in the classroom, and also acts as a communication tool for administrators and parents. Teachers who take the time to write detailed goals and plans demonstrate a willingness to be accountable for classroom activity. A first-year teacher was recently able to convince her principal and, subsequently, the administration and parents, of the strengths of shifting to a multi-age program because of the carefully thought-out plan that she had presented. This plan included clear overall goals, how the state's many and detailed grade-level competencies were to be met in a more developmentally appropriate way, and a holistic plan for meeting these goals.

Learning Experiences

The main purpose of planning is to make school, lessons, and activities meet the needs of children. If these needs are not met, the frequent result is behavior that is not wanted both inside and outside of the classroom. Children learn very early how to "turn off" and "tune out" if the experience does not fit into their cognitive schema. What is planned, therefore, is not only the general overview for the year, but monthly goals and specific daily activities to meet those goals. It is these daily learning experiences that must be growth activities with holding power for the child if gains and growth are to be made. *Growth activities* are those learning experiences that permit a child to return to the basic concept or core of the experience frequently throughout the year, each time exploring the activity in a more knowing and sophisticated way. *Holding power* entails structuring those experiences so that all children in the class can work at their own level. Suggestions for such extensions and increased complexity are always included in well-thought-out plans.

A good example of a growth activity with holding power that also lends itself to extensions is geoboards. A geoboard (short for geometry board) is a ten-inch by ten-inch board with twenty-five nails spaced two inches apart, starting in one inch from the edge of the board.

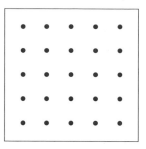

Rubber bands are stretched around the nails to create geometric shapes of all kinds. Primary school-age children need to have ample time to explore the board, experimenting with different shapes: all kinds of squares, rectangles, triangles, and quadrilaterals. Teachers need to remember that to a preoperational child, if it looks different, it is different; hence the reference to "all kinds" of shapes. Placement on the geoboard can cause a primary school-age child to be convinced that the following shapes are, indeed, "different":

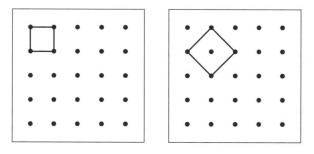

Being able to reproduce shapes on geoboard paper gives another level of sophistication and difficulty. Just having the geoboards with rubber bands available, will "get old" very fast, resulting in either the children totally ignoring the materials after the first couple of days, or engaging in inappropriate behavior, such as shooting rubber bands off the nails. With the addition of geoboard paper for drawing shapes, children can extend these initial explorations into reproducing their work on the board onto paper. This activity not only improves hand/eye coordination but gives the teacher clues and cues as to how children are developing their visual-spatial intelligence. For instance, does the child find a "beginning nail" and follow the rubber band from nail to nail to draw the shape, counting each nail and its position on the board? Does the child just draw the shape in a holistic fashion, seemingly having a mental picture of the shape in his or her head? Does the child reproduce the shape correctly, but in another location on the board? Just by adding geoboard paper, some straightedges, and pencils, the original geoboard activity becomes more complex and provides an extension of the initial exploration.

With the further addition of two-inch paper squares cut from construction paper, older children (eight-, nine-, and ten-year-olds) can extend their work further by finding areas and solving such problems as, "how many different shapes can you build on your geoboard that have exactly three squares inside?" Each shape should be transferred to geoboard paper, and the paper squares cut and glued into place on the paper to prove the area. This problem can be repeated and further extended by changing the number of squares, or area, being targeted.

A rule for determining whether a learning experience has holding power is to watch what children do with any new material and activity that has been added to the environment. Questions for the teacher to ask in the planning process should include:

1. Does the activity "hold" only the children who are very focused and inquisitive?
2. For what period of time will the activity hold the interest of different levels of learners?
3. What do the children do with the materials and other work suggestions?
4. Are children using the materials in ways other than those the teacher intended, but which are great ideas?
5. Are children exhibiting disruptive and inappropriate behavior?
6. If children are using materials inappropriately, is it due to *how* the workspace is provisioned, *where* in the room the workspace is located, or both?

If materials are not visible, they will not be used. If all of the needed materials are not in place, not much beyond an initial experimentation will occur. Careful consideration of all details of the desired learning experiences is a critical component of planning and organization.

A triangular framework, on page 136, with a very broad base helps in the decision-making process for provisioning learning experiences. The base of the triangle depicts the primary ages: the five-, six-, and seven-year-olds, for whom the focus of work is *experiential* and *exploratory*. The second level of the triangle illustrates the intermediate ages: the eight-, nine-, and ten-year-olds, whose work is characterized by an *awareness* of their advancing concepts, skills, and thinking begun in the primary experiences. These children are beginning to make the connections between what they are learning and the real world, between school and community. As Gardner points out, a child of this age is curious about and ready to learn the symbol systems of his or her culture. The apex of the triangle is for the eleven-, twelve-, and thirteen-year-olds (the middle school in many communities

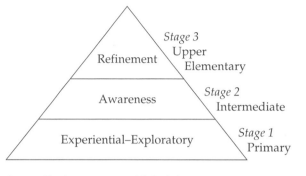

Source: Charbonneau, unpublished dissertation

today). At this level, the focus becomes *refinement* of what has been learned previously, especially through the use of projects and apprenticeships.

Strategies for Achieving Planned Objectives

Two important aspects of the planning process must always be considered: the role of other adults in the classroom and instructional strategies for achieving planned objectives. Both impact the desired outcomes.

Roles of the Adult or Adults

Instructional leadership can be in the hands of: (1) the single teacher in the classroom, (2) a teacher and an instructional assistant, (3) a teacher and parent volunteers, or (4) a team teaching effort which is often the situation in multi-age classrooms. It is important to determine who will be responsible for what. In the case of instructional assistants as well as parent volunteers, they must understand and believe in "less is more"—the philosophy which undergirds the integrated classroom as well as Sizer's Re:Learning techniques. They must learn when to help directly and when to act as a catalyst and a resource; they must understand the use of materials and what children are expected to do for themselves. It often is helpful to have an assistant work with just one of two areas of the room until he or she becomes very familiar with operating procedures and instructional goals and strategies. It does not help to have an assistant tell a child specifically what to do and how to do it if the entire learning experience was a problem-solving one! Clearly it is important to plan directly with all of the adults involved in a particular classroom so that everyone knows exactly what is expected from the learning experience.

Team Teaching

Team teaching, with its potential to draw on the unique strengths of two or three individuals, can definitely enhance the overall program of a classroom as well as provide a way to share the task of planning the complex theme studies and individualized experiences needed in an integrated approach. Team teaching also helps in the area of provisioning, as each teacher can then take the responsibility for provisioning specific workspaces and learning experiences. Team teaching often occurs when two or more classrooms have been put together, resulting in greater numbers of children using a larger space. This, again, calls for clearly designated parameters for each team member in overseeing daily activities.

Another form of team teaching can be used in the planning process rather than in curriculum delivery when a school has several multi-age classrooms at the same level. This type of "teaming" is done to assure that the long-term goals and objectives for each of the comparable groups are basically the same, and the learning experiences designed to reach those goals provide children with appropriate concepts and skills. While each team member might approach the objectives somewhat differently given the children in his or her particular group, the overall curriculum content is comparable and comprehensive. This form of team teaching is another way for teachers to share ideas, individual strengths, materials, and insights. Sharing "what works" and "what doesn't work" can save hours of time and frustration.

Working as a team carries the special responsibility for each member of contributing equally to the design and implementation of the collective effort. It is therefore very important that members of the team are compatible, harmonious, and cooperative. The increased stress of a discordant team puts an additional burden on any teacher.

Instructional Strategies

Teachers plan instructional strategies to be used at particular times and with particular learning experiences. Decisions are made about the best method of instruction for a particular goal or objective, as well as for creating the optimal learning environment for a group of children or an individual child. The instructional strategies to be considered are: (1) large group, appropriate when beginning and ending theme studies and projects, (2) small groups, the optimum environment for direct teaching of needed skills and concepts, (3) pairs of children, a situation that works especially well with younger children in inquiry and problem solving across the content areas, and with older children who either share the same interests or who want to investigate the same topics, (4) experiential/experimental learning experiences with no specific planned outcomes, (5) discovery sessions in which the activities and learning experiences are planned so that something specific is to be learned, (6) inquiry, in which the focus is on recognizing and formulating the problem, as well as planning and organizing for its solution, (7) cooperative learning, a setting that has several successful formats contingent upon the desired outcomes, (8) critical thinking, which pervades all activities, and (9) research, a skill all children can learn effectively if started early on with appropriate resources and recording choices.

Interrelationship Between Content Areas

Teachers need to understand the interrelationships between subject areas that, on the surface, do not seem related: for example, mathematics and writing. In 1989, the National Council of Teachers of Mathematics published a landmark document entitled Curriculum and Evaluation Standards for School Mathematics, which carefully describes standards for each of three levels in school mathematics: kindergarten through grade 4, grades 5 through 8, and grades 9 through 12. The first four standards at each level are identical:

1. *Mathematics as problem solving*
2. *Mathematics as communication*
3. *Mathematics as reasoning*
4. *Mathematical connections*

Having children write about mathematics is still very difficult for teachers to facilitate and for children to understand. Keeping a mathematical journal can be as helpful for children as it can be for teachers. If children have a way and a place to describe what they are doing, detailing their successes as well as their difficulties, writing about mathematical experiences becomes less frightening . If children can do this, they are well on their way to developing intrapersonal strategies that can advance their learning. Writing about math increases the probability that children will understand mathematics as more than arithmetic skills. Mathematical investigations cover a wide range of topics and concepts. Through writing about math, children can discover problem-solving strategies that will allow for experimentation and exploration of different ways of reaching a solution, as well as represent that solution in words and pictures. Asking children to write about how they solved a problem helps to clarify their thinking and underscores the necessity for communicating with others in ways that can be easily understood. In addition, having children write about their experiences with mathematics not only provides clarification and insight for the child, but also provides information for the teacher in his or her ongoing planning process.

While small group direct teaching can lessen the possibility of missing some child's misunderstanding, having children write about a lesson can point up strengths and weaknesses in individual thinking, concepts, and strategies. Good questions for the teacher to ask might include:

1. Tell me what you learned this morning about finding the area of triangles?
2. What was hard for you when you searched for prime numbers between zero and one hundred?
3. How did you begin to think about creating a winning strategy for the game we played?
4. Tell me why you decided to change your strategy when using the rods to find the volume of the containers?
5. You stated that you thought that any triangle is always half the area of a given rectangle. How can you prove or disprove your theory?

Erin's Journal

A sample of a ten-year-old's first exploration into the more formal world of fractions is demonstrated by the following problem:

Erin was asked to share six cookies equally with seven children (Cohen, 1988). Erin had worked with various manipulative materials and with real-world measuring tools, using some of the easier common fractions. This was Erin's first attempt at tackling a problem without teacher support. Writing about how she got her results was not a new experience, which is evident by how clearly she presents her ideas. Erin shared her solution to the cookie problem with the class and her teacher (see pages 140–141).

A few mornings later Erin arrived at school with an additional page of "thinking."(see page 142)

There was no doubt in Erin's teacher's mind that Erin had, indeed, assimilated an important fractional concept for herself, and that Erin was able to communicate her knowledge to others in a comprehensive and meaningful way. Not only did Erin's writing of her strategy help her thinking, but it also gave her teacher an understanding of her mathematical development. Erin had tied mathematics to writing in an interesting way; communicating with drawings, words, and charts.

Erin
(age 10)

My problem is to share 6 cookies equally between 7 kids. First I made 6 chocolate chip cookies from construction paper. Don' t they look good?

Then I decided that I would have to cut each one in half to start the sharing.

That left 5 half cookies. I cut the halfs in half like this:

Now I have 3 pieces left that are like quarters When I cut

②

those in half I didn't have
enough to share out ↓

⊕   so I have to
cut again like

this: and I can
do it again for the rest of the
pieces. So each kid gets another
piece — probably crumbs.
Then I have to say how much
each kid got:

⊂| a half   ⊂| a quarter   ◁ a sixteen
                                   I think

and some crumbs.

Erin

Last night I thought about my cookie problem.
I thought I saw a pattern. When I cut
each piece in
half, it goes

started with	ended with	
◯	$\frac{1}{2}$	→2
⬭	$\frac{1}{4}$	→4
◇	$\frac{1}{8}$	→8
◹	$\frac{1}{16}$	→16
◹	$\frac{1}{32}$	→32
	(the crumbs!)	

If I could cut again, I bet the
next size would be $\frac{1}{64}$ wouldn't it?

Each part is 1 out of how many equal pieces
you make isn't it? (Tell me if
I'm right please)

Problem Solving Across the Curriculum

Providing opportunities for problem solving across content areas encourages children to look for interrelationships. Erin was able to see the connection between mathematical reasoning, language, and clear communication. Problem solving across the curriculum also encourages long-term investigations that are not facilitated by traditionally segmented work times. Time blocks must be long enough for children to utilize concepts and skills in a variety of ways in their problem-solving processes, providing opportunities for communicating through different representations and presentations. The more traditional time periods afforded for activities tend to encourage more fragmented, superficial thinking. Learning in such a situation focuses on isolated skills rather than a holistic integration. Children require time to reflect on their solutions and strategies so that they become more knowledgeable about their own learning process and more capable of making good decisions when they approach new tasks. As children problem solve across content areas, interrelationships become apparent. Children experience how mathematics, reading and writing, science, and social studies can all overlap and intersect. They also learn how to bring various disciplines into the problem-solving situation in a natural way.

For example, making a map involves visual-spatial skills, an understanding of scale, understanding of proportion and measurement, drawing, and knowledge of land and water forms. Research for a map-making project includes the use of almanacs, atlases, geography books, mathematics resources and books related to the topic of the map, as well as computer programs and video disks. An exciting short theme topic for such a project might be the Oregon Trail, its history and use.

Multiple Approaches to a Theme Study

A group of eight-, nine-, and ten-year-olds have been studying the westward expansion of the United States. One history book that a pair of children had been researching gave an exciting account of one family's journey across the Oregon Trail. This account fascinated the children and they decided to draw a map of the trail with all of the main physical features, forts, and trading posts. In their research, they needed to determine the total length of the trail, and the appropriate scale to use to draw the trail. The children also needed to study previously drawn maps so that they could correctly locate where the trail was located, and the distances between safe stopping places. They also needed to include in their map rivers, mountains, and other physical features that were found along the Oregon Trail. The children then discussed at length the problems that

(continued)

(continued)

the travelers along the trail faced as they made their long journey.This research and reading prompted several children to write their own versions of these problems and their solutions. Enhancing their own study was the use of a well-known computer disk called The Oregon Trail (Minnesota Educational Computing Consortium), which allowed them to simulate the journey and practice a variety of decision-making skills.

The process of learning requires an involvement of children in relevant experiences where there is activity, purpose, and anticipated outcomes leading to additional relevant experiences and anticipated outcomes. It is a cycle that is ongoing, and requires participation of both the teacher and the children. Meaningful learning occurs on multiple levels. Children learn content and skills and, often more importantly, they learn to think about their thinking. This enables the child to approach new learning experiences with knowledge about self, about problem solving, and about using specific strategies and unique combinations of intelligences according to task demands. The teacher may not be as visible in this setting as in the traditional classroom. However, he or she is the major force that drives the classroom. As facilitator, observer, coach, and planner, the teacher is actively involved in creating a learning environment that is supportive to each child. In addition, important factors such as the development of social competency, independence, and overall problem-solving skills increase the resiliency factors which help to prevent at-risk behaviors (The Western Regional Center, 1991).

Suggested Activities

Observations and activities that can enhance the teacher's ability to plan for meaningful learning are:

1. Observing children using a variety of manipulative materials.
2. Questioning children about their thinking processes and strategies.
3. Listening to children brainstorming a project or theme study in cooperation with other children.
4. Involving the children in the planning process.
5. Involving children in the evaluation of the total learning experience.
6. Utilizing children's interests as the basis for integrated research projects.

By using the above cited techniques frequently, teachers can make more informed decisions about goals and objectives, long- and short-term learning activities, concept areas that need exploring and refining, as well as specific skills that each child needs to succeed.

References

Cohen, Don. (1988). *Calculus by and for Young People*. Illinois: The Mathematician.

Gamberg, Ruth, Kwak, Winniefred, Hutchings, Meredith, and Altheim, Judy. (1988). *Learning and Loving It*. New Hampshire: Heinemann Educational Books, Inc.

Gardner, Howard. (1991). *The Unschooled Mind*. New York: Basic Books.

Gardner, Howard. (1993). *Multiple Intelligences: The Theory in Practice*. New York: Basic Books.

Goodman, Yetta. (1978). Kid-Watching, an Alternative to Testing. *National Elementary Principal*, 57(4), 41–45.

Western Regional Center: Drug Free Schools and Communities. (1991). *Fostering Resliancy: Protective Factors in the Family, School and Community*.

Yeomans, Edward. (1969). *The Wellsprings of Teaching*. Boston: National Association of Independent School.

7

A Multiple Approach to an Integrated Classroom: Theory to Practice

The important thing is not that every child should be taught, but that every child should be given the wish to learn. (John Lubbock)

No "One Right Way"

One of the greatest strengths of the integrated classroom is that it lends itself to a variety of implementations within the philosophy. Regardless of how a teacher approaches the integrated classroom, all such classrooms incorporate the following:

1. Developmental appropriateness for the age group.
2. An environment which supports success for all children.
3. Multi-age (family, vertical) grouping.
4. Joint goal setting between teacher and student that takes into consideration the specific concerns of the community.
5. Relevant, active learning experiences.
6. A well-provisioned environment that encourages independence.
7. The careful development of multiple intelligences.
8. Opportunities for children to develop skills and attitudes that promote resiliency.
9. High expectations for all children.
10. Ongoing formal and informal assessment of children, teachers, and curriculum.

Methods of implementation of the integrated curriculum can include one or more varied instructional strategies, which can change and expand according to each situation. Because there is such flexibility in how the integrated classroom can be approached, teachers can make changes gradually depending on their previous experience, the children's previous experiences and reactions, and the responses of the administration and parents. Approaches include integration of time, subjects, or both, theme studies, and specific activities that lend themselves to an integration of skills addressing different intelligences, personalized instruction, differential groupings of children, and using different methodologies for the investigation of subject matter.

Time as the Integrating Factor

When time is the integrating factor, the boundaries that constrain the traditional classroom are removed. Children are free, within clearly delineated guidelines, to take as much or as little time as needed to work on specific subject areas or activities within a given day. Time frames for accomplishing certain tasks are not limited: for some children this means the privilege of returning to an unfinished project over a span of time. Children must understand what is required of them on a daily basis and that these requirements are jointly determined by student and teacher. Children are not asked to work on the same activity at the same time. In one classroom there may be children engaged in science investigations, reading and writing experiences, and mathematical inquiry, all at the same time. Subject content might not always cross over disciplines or be directly related to an ongoing project, but there are no isolated assignments or skill drills which fragment learning.

One highly successful primary integrated classroom required that children be responsible for activities related to words and numbers on a daily basis. Each child in this group of five-, six-, and seven-year-olds knew that he or she needed to do something with words and something with numbers every day. Although this approach may sound very narrow, it was not. *Words* can encompass reading, silent or shared, on any topic or area, listening to and writing stories, essays, research, letters, questions, labels, journals, and reports, spelling practice using newly learned words in a variety of ways, vocabulary study and extensions, publishing prose or poetry, utilizing a tape recorder for listening or speaking, and using a video camera to record a performance. *Numbers* can include simple counting activities and building with Cuisenaire rods, taking surveys on topics which can be graphed or represented pictorially, exploring probability, estimation and measurement activities, and real-world problem solving, practicing skills, and planning for experiences that require mathematical reasoning. On a daily basis, children determined with the help of the teacher what they expected to accomplish with words and numbers. The completed work was presented to the teacher in some form. The child or a more experienced peer then noted the child's activity on a large chart which specified WORDS or NUMBERS.

For the teacher who is new to this approach, using two distinct time frames in a morning can help with transitioning from a traditional classroom to a more integrated one. For instance, the first half of the morning can be devoted to numbers and the second half to words. The same kind of time distribution can be used for other subjects as well. It must be emphasized that within these time frames and subject areas, children are working on different activities or projects.

Integrating Subjects

Teachers who do not choose to integrate both time and subjects may designate specific time periods for subject areas that seem to them to be related. Those subjects that are most easily integrated include mathematics and science, and literacy and social studies. Art, music, physical education, and dance can all become part of any subject area.

Different Ways To Consider Integrating Subjects

Heidi Hayes Jacobs suggests that, when examining the relationship between fields of knowledge, the following can be considered:

> **Crossdisciplinary:** *viewing one discipline from the perspective of another; for example, the physics of music and the history of math.*
>
> **Multidisciplinary:** *the juxtaposition of several disciplines focused on one problem with no attempt to integrate.*
>
> **Pluridisciplinary:** *the juxtaposition assumed to be more or less related; for example, math and physics, French and Latin.*
>
> **Transdisciplinary:** *beyond the scope of the disciplines; that is, to start with a problem and bring to bear knowledge from the disciplines.* (Jacobs, 1989, p. 8)

While these are very specific definitions that help in understanding how curriculum can be shaped, Jacobs prefers the term *interdisciplinary* and gives the following definition: "a knowledge view and curriculum approach that consciously applies methodology and language from more than one discipline to examine a central theme, issue, problem, topic, or experience"(p. 8).

Jacobs' book is very helpful to those who have limited experience with the concepts of integration: what it is, what it can do for learners of all ages, and how it can be created and implemented, depending on one's goals and objectives.

Theme Studies

A theme study integrates subjects around a particular focus or topic of interest. According to Gamberg, Kwak, Hutchings and Altheim (1988), the characteristics of a theme study include an in-depth study of a particular topic; it must be of interest to children, and be broad enough to be divided into smaller subtopics. The relationship of the subtopics to the wider topic must remain clear. The topic should not be geographically or historically limiting; and the topic should lend itself to comparing and contrasting ideas as well as foster extensive investigation of concrete situations, materials, and resources. Theme studies remove the barriers that maintain specific knowledge and skills within particular subjects, as well as the separation of the classroom from the larger community. *Learning and Loving it,* a detailed book on generating and implementing good theme studies by Gamberg et al., is an invaluable source for teachers who are beginning to use the theme study approach, as well as for those who have some experience with themes.

Some topics that would make good theme studies include content areas such as oceans, world fishing, architecture, games and children around the world, fibers, clothing, animals, insects, issues such as environmental protection and the ethical use of the media, and those topics posed by "essential questions" (Sizer: Coalition of Essential Schools). Some examples of essential questions are: (1) Power—what is the nature of power? Who makes decisions? Can power be bought or sold? What is the relationship between order and power? (2) What is worth knowing? and (3) Who is an American?

Theme studies should not be contrived to include subject disciplines that do not readily fit. It is sometimes necessary to make sure that these areas are addressed at other times of the day or week. Theme studies take place over an extended period of time, offering many opportunities for different kinds of investigations and representations. Theme studies require that children work cooperatively in groups as well as individually and that there be a culminating shared experience at the end of the study. Successful schools that use theme studies suggest a maximum of three over a year's time.

Integrating Activities

A good way to begin an integrated approach is to choose specific activities that lend themselves to an integration of skills and intelligences. Many activities that occur in the classroom would fit this category, providing the teacher is clear on the potential outcomes. What is critical is to be sure that the activities offered to the children embody the use of whatever skills the teacher wants the children to use or practice at any given time.

Some good integrating activities are: bookmaking, papermaking, construction with wood and/or junk materials, cooking experiences, many art and music projects, growing plants, caring for pets, and strategy games. Bookmaking, for example, requires reading and processing instructions, following directions, planning and organizing, measuring, and using tools and different kinds of materials. Actually creating the book can take place before or after the contents of the book are created. Children frequently like to collect all of the stories they have written into one volume, or bind together all of their mathematical investigations on geoboards. An integrating activity such as bookmaking may stimulate a child to search out additional information that would incorporate still other skills, concepts, and thought processes.

Personalizing Instruction

Personalizing instruction requires that individual children or small groups of children work on different activities or projects throughout the day. Embedded in these projects are the needed skills and concepts that the teacher has determined are appropriate at this time for each child.

The basis of personalized instruction is the teacher's knowledge of where each child is in his or her learning profile. This requires an ongoing assessment of the child's participation with peers, his or her ability to act as a responsible learner, and his or her understanding of concepts and content. One method of personalizing instruction particularly successful in the integrated setting is the use of contracts.

Contracts in the Integrated Classroom

Marge Jones, who teaches a multi-age first-, second-, and third-grade classroom in the Santa Fe Public School system, has created a system of contracting as well as a series of contracts to meet differing needs both cognitively and socially.

At the beginning of the school year, Ms. Jones creates five multi-age groups from the total group of children. Each group is then assigned one area or workspace of the classroom to investigate in depth: what materials are there and what possible uses can be made of these materials. The group decides together on possible uses/projects that could be explored and makes a chart to share with the entire class at a later time. Each group is then rotated into another area to repeat the process. A workspace might contain microscopes, hand lenses, different kinds of paper and recording tools, boxes of rocks, leaves, insects, fibers, salt, sugar, flour, cornstarch, and other items for observation under a microscope or hand lens. Another area might contain games from around the world, costumes and clothing from other countries, story

(continued)

(continued)

books and reference material about other countries, and recording tools. A third workspace might include blueprints, blocks, boxes and other "junk" materials for building, maps of the community, and books on construction of all kinds. A fourth area could have a microwave oven, a crockpot, cookbooks, a full complement of measuring spoons and cups, and appropriate cooking and eating utensils. A fifth area might include a multitude of books, magazines, other information sources such as pamphlets, a listening center, tape recordings, a computer, a typewriter, writing paper, pencils, pens, crayons, markers, and bookmaking materials including poster card, matte board, tape, a bookbinding stapler, and so on. There are also baskets of books, paper, writing and drawing materials, scissors, glue, etc., in every area. Many of these are brought in by the children, which helps give them a feeling of ownership in the classroom. The purpose of the rotation through the areas is to initiate new children into group work, to acquaint students with where materials are located in the classroom, and to generate ideas.

At the end of the first two days of school, Ms. Jones and her students have a collection of ideas that can be pursued at each workspace. The children who have been with Ms. Jones previously already know the procedure for contracting and working independently, and do so beginning the very next day. The youngest children are guided through the process of contracting gradually over the first few months of the school year. Children are first encouraged to make simple choices as to a project or activity to take place in a particular area. Children agree, with Ms. Jones, on what they are going to do, what their plans are for accomplishing their tasks and what time period they will accomplish their tasks in. This initial "contract" is dictated to Ms. Jones who then represents it both in words and pictures for the child. Each child is expected to follow his or her plan, and Ms. Jones meets with each child on a daily basis to assess his or her progress. As these younger children become more and more responsible, they are able to choose projects that require a longer time period to complete. As they become more familiar with the contracting process, they may decide to do joint contracting with another child or small group. At the beginning of the winter term, these younger children select their contracts from the choices offered to the older children.

Another opportunity for learning responsibility for contracting in Ms. Jones' classroom is through the use of theme studies involving the whole class. Small groups of children, regardless of age, select a subtopic of the theme to research. This becomes the basis for each group's contract with the teacher and the rest of the class. The younger children, then, are able to observe good models for decision making and planning, as well as formation and execution of the contract.

Examples of contracts found in Ms. Jones classroom can be found on pages 153–156.

Contract A

Name _____   _   Date _____

Book and skill card _____

_____

Share a book (English and Spanish) _____

_____

_____

Game or drill _____

_____

_____

Group drama _____

_____

_____

Research project _____

_____

_____

My best work and why_____

_____

This could have been better and how _____

_____

Contract B

Name _____   Date _____

Community or environment helper _____

_____

_____

Group book_____

_____

_____

Math project _____

_____

_____

(continued)

(continued)

Science experiment _____

_____

_____

Group Spanish activity _____

_____

_____

Best work _____
Why _____
Needs help _____

Contract C

Name _____   Date _____

Grade

_____   Read and record _____

_____

_____

_____   Book report II _____

_____

_____

_____   Survey and graph _____

_____

_____

_____   Write a letter _____

_____

_____

_____   Group debate _____

Grade Chart   _✓_ wonderful
              _✗_ alright
              _0_ could be better

Contract D

Name _____   Date _____

Measurement project _____

_____

_____

Book report I_____

_____

Make up your own activities

Subject _____   _____

1. _____

_____

_____

2. _____

_____

_____

3. _____

_____

_____

I like this contract_____I didn't like this contract_____

because _____

_____

Contract E

Name _____   Date_____

Listening and activity (may be Spanish) _____

_____

_____

Book and skill card _____

_____

_____

Math game _____

_____

_____

Group bulletin board _____

_____

_____

Share and outline a science book _____

_____

_____

I liked this _____

because _____

(continued)

(continued)

This was not great _____

because _____

Contract F

Name _____   Date _____

Book and skill card _____
_____
_____

Cuisenaire cards _____
_____
_____

Money or time project _____
_____
_____

Community poster or activity _____
_____
_____

Translate spanish book _____
_____
_____

Number from best _____1_____ to not so good _____5_____

In her classroom, Ms. Jones relies heavily on older, more experienced children to help the younger children to negotiate the environment. Having children over a period of three years ensures that there will be enough children who understand the contracting process well enough to assist those who are just learning the process. However, young children in single-age classrooms can learn how to contract if the teacher provides instruction, practice, and consistency, and recognizes that more time may be needed to make this a successful experience.

An approach focusing on the multiple intelligences is another way of personalizing instruction. This requires that the classroom be provisioned to support each of these intelligences and that teachers observe children carefully as they make choices and carry out projects. Such a classroom would have an area with musical instruments, tape recorders for listening to music, singing along, or playing along with the music, paper for writing music, and song books. Another area might be one to support linguistic intelligence and include such things as books, writing materials, stories on tape, tape recorders for dictation, and computers for word processing. When children tend to avoid a particular area, such as linguistics, the teacher can encourage and support specific work in this area by working directly with the child, pairing the child with another child whose strength is in this area, or by contracting with a child for a particular activity in this area. This same child might exhibit particular strength in visual-spatial intelligence, for example, through art. Encouraging the child to use his or her artistic ability to illustrate his or her stories helps the child to see the connection between the intelligences, and supports the child's strengths while building those intelligences that are less developed. As with contracting, utilizing the multiple intelligences as a way of designing curriculum usually requires that each child work on activities and projects that are different from the activities and projects of another child.

Getting Started

The Teacher

Many teachers find that it is easier to make the shift slowly from a traditional classroom to an integrated one. In order for a teacher to be successful in this process he or she must have two basic beliefs: (1) children, when given the opportunity, can and want to direct their own learning process, and (2) power regarding classroom decisions can and should be shared with children. If the teacher takes the position that children will only learn if there are adequate external rewards and that all decisions must be made solely by the teacher, the integrated approach is bound to fail. A slow shift enables the teacher to observe how children are responding, and possibly more importantly, how the teacher him- or herself is responding. Continual reflection and evaluation is necessary if the teacher is to be successful. A teacher new to this method may give up too easily because it is so different from the way that teacher was taught as a child. In addition, the teacher may not have had any training in this method or adequate role models in his or her teacher training program.

A slow start may mean trying the integrated approach one morning a week initially and then adding activities, materials, and more time, building on successful experiences. Another way to get started is to begin with a theme study, which again, takes place during only a part of the day. When using this approach it is important to use other time frames in the day to cover subject areas that do not lend themselves naturally to the theme.

The Environment

Using the theme study approach minimizes the need for drastic change in the physical structure of the room. Desks can easily be rearranged into small groups or pairs depending on the investigations taking place. Necessary materials can be provided in various locations easily accessible to the children. Library research and community resources can be included as part of the program, thereby expanding the boundaries of the classroom. As teachers experiment with the theme study approach, they may find that they wish to build and expand the theme study to involve more time, more permanent workspaces, and more individualized activities within these workspaces.

Having a limited number of permanent workspaces may be another interim step on the road to fully integrating the classroom. With this approach, the teacher must be especially careful not to make the workspace activity a reward for finishing prescribed work, or use the workspace to provide extra drill and practice worksheets. A good beginning workspace might be for bookmaking, where children can take collections of their written work in any subject area and learn how to bind it into a readable book. This space also could be a "library" of children's work to be shared with others. Another simple initial workspace could be used for observation and recording observations such as the growth and development of plants and animals, specific collections of objects for viewing under a microscope, and gathering weather data and graphing weather changes. A space by the window can provide a means to observe nature as it naturally unfolds throughout the seasons. For any workspace to be successful, the teacher must anticipate what materials children will need and provide them. In addition, challenging questions, books, and resources that will stimulate investigation, as well as inviting pictures and posters concerning the topic, all placed at the children's eye level, will help to ensure that children will use the space in a productive way. It also can be very helpful to provide display space in the area for children to post their findings and exhibit their projects.

As the teacher becomes more comfortable with this approach, he or she may design the environment to be supportive of a totally integrated classroom. This requires doing away with desks in rows or even clusters, and provisioning the classroom as described in Chapter 3.

Curriculum Resource

A successful beginning for a teacher using the integrated approach requires choosing curriculum for initial themes, workspaces, or both that are interesting and exciting for both the teacher and the children. The curriculum should offer many opportunities for integrating time, subjects, and individual needs. The teacher should take the time to plan carefully with goals and objectives clearly in mind for the whole class as well as for individual children. To assure interest, curriculum should reflect the real world, helping children make connections between school, themselves, and their community. For the teacher, curriculum should be easily translated into the competencies required by individual schools and parents, or the larger district/state policies.

There are curricula already published that lend themselves to the beginning steps towards integration. Elementary Science Study units currently available through Delta Education Company are basically science-oriented investigations that call for research into the topic itself as well as related fields. These units ask that children represent their learning in multiple ways: writing both questions and answers, drawing, charting, graphing, and using the skills from many disciplines. Some titles include the *Musical Instrument Recipe Booklet* (building and using musical instruments), *Peas and Particles* (estimating and counting huge numbers of items), and *Cardboard Carpentry* (constructing furniture and storage units from triwall). Each teacher's guide provides extensions into connected subject areas such as mathematics or social studies.

The AIMS project (Activities in Math and Science) emphasizes the connections between mathematics and science and has extensive units of study for both primary and upper elementary grades, as well as the middle grades. More and more materials that connect science and mathematics are finding their way to the marketplace, given the guidelines published by the National Council of Teachers of Mathematics (NCTM) and the National Science Teachers Association (NSTA), which emphasize the integration of content areas as much as possible. Another such integrated mathematics/science project is GEMS (Great Explorations in Math and Science), which has been developed at the Lawrence Hall of Science, University of California at Berkeley. Both AIMS and GEMS emphasize the need for interdisciplinary studies, and incorporate several subject area skills and concepts into their units. The American Association for the Advancement of Science has published guidelines entitled "Project 2061," sometimes referred to as "Science for All Americans," which also underscores the need to use an interdisciplinary approach.

Future Problem Solving is another curriculum which crosses content areas by having children think deeply about and research solutions to world issues. Future Problem Solving is a year-long program in which teams of four children use a six-step problem-solving process to analyze and offer solutions to complex scientific and social problems of the future. During the year's time, children work on three problems, which are mailed to evaluators for scoring and feedback. This evaluation provides reinforcement for clear thinking and suggestions for improvement on each step of the process. This program focuses on developing higher-level thinking skills, which improves communication, requires working cooperatively with teammates, teaches about complex societal issues, and develops research skills. The problem-solving process requires both convergent and divergent thinking, as students brainstorm many problems related to the main topic, identify one good underlying problem, and brainstorm solutions to this underlying problem. The students must develop criteria by which to judge their solutions, and evaluate each solution to determine the best one. Each of the topics cover a wide range of scientific and social concerns. Some of the recently assigned topics have been global warming, acid rain, the American legal system, terrorism, nutrition, poverty, education, the elderly, the arms race, and immigration. Future Problem Solving is structured into four levels: primary (grades K-1-2-3), junior (grades 4-5-6), intermediate (grades 7-8-9) and senior (grades 10-11-12). For information on this program, contact the Future Problem Solving Program, 318 West Ann Avenue, Ann Arbor, Michigan 48104-1337, (313) 998-7FPS.

Two outstanding integrated studies for fourth grade and up are "The Voyage of the Mimi" and "The Second Voyage of the Mimi." These materials include videotapes, study guides, extension possibilities, computer software, background materials, and posters which focus on whales and their environment (Voyage of the Mimi) and archeological explorations (Second Voyage of the Mimi). These two integrated studies, although created by the Bank Street College Project in Science and Mathematics, can be obtained from Wings For Learning, a division of Sunburst Publications.

Another good source of information is *An Integrated Language Perspective in the Elementary School* (Pappas, Kiefer, and Levstik, 1990) which provides examples of how to develop a theme study, examples of some theme studies for different age levels, and considerable resources primarily in the area of literature which support the theme.

In looking for ready-made integrated studies, the teacher should be aware that some published studies tend to be shallow in content and delivery, using the integrated approach in a superficial manner. Activities may seem contrived and connections forced. There may not be a clear connection to the real world, and critical thinking, as well as comparing and contrasting ideas may not be encouraged.

In many schools, textbooks drive the curriculum. Texts can be instrumental in helping to define curriculum content, but in the integrated classroom they should be viewed as only one source of available material. Textbooks, by their very nature, often limit the teacher's thinking about what is possible for his or her students. They frequently suggest rigid approaches with narrow outcomes geared to an artificial developmental level, such as specific content for a specific grade. For a teacher who wants to move away from texts slowly, we suggest that every two weeks the teacher select a subject area for which no texts will be used. In place of the text, for that two-week period, the teacher creates the unit of study, gathering resources from various books and materials. Within the unit of study, the teacher includes a number of different methods of evaluating student outcomes, as well as many opportunities to reflect on the successes and limitations of how the teacher has chosen to implement the unit. The process of reflection provides the teacher with specific information as to what exactly needs to be modified or changed to ensure that the next unit of study will be more successful. It is important that teachers recognize that any new method of teaching/learning requires persistence, and that failures can be a positive part of the change and growth process. Continued success with these brief two-week creative endeavors can encourage the teacher to try longer periods of time, two or more subject areas within the given period of time, or both.

Grouping

How children are grouped at any given time in the integrated classroom is dependent on the goals for a particular project or lesson. A strength of the integrated classroom is its variety of developmental levels because of the multi-age grouping. Children whose cognitive development is more advanced can be called upon to mentor other children whose cognition is not as developed. For the more advanced child, this provides opportunities to learn material in a more complex way, taking the perspective of the teacher to make explanations that can be understood by the less advanced peer. The less advanced peer is often more receptive to a peer teacher than to an adult. The less advanced peer's concepts are challenged by the mentor, and appropriate scaffolding is provided.

Socially, the more advanced peers provide a model for behavior, social problem solving, and group interactions. The less advanced peers challenge their mentors to be more reflective concerning their behavior and interactions, given their responsibility as leaders in the classroom. Cooperative learning activities can also be strengthened by placing together children whose developmental levels, both cognitive and social-emotional, are complementary. Children, then, can challenge each other's perspectives, model varying strengths for each other, and provide experiences which allow for new ways of thinking and problem solving. Grouping children across developmental levels also supports the teacher in his or her work with small groups and individual children, by using the more advanced children to help maintain focus for those less advanced. It is crucial that the teacher have many opportunities to spend time with individual children, especially those that are often "missed" because they are not demanding of the teacher's attention. In many classrooms, these are the children who are not at the top or the bottom of the developmental hierarchy, but rather somewhere in the middle. These children perform at a satisfactory level, but frequently are not challenged to go beyond what is considered acceptable.

It is a given that the teacher must also work with the more advanced children, helping them to develop the skills and the sense of responsibility necessary for them to take on this role of teacher to peers. The benefit of the inclusion of these children into the teaching role promotes feelings of social competence, responsibility for others, and independence; all factors that support resiliency in the face of at-risk situations. The same benefits apply to the less advanced peer as he or she learns new ways of behaving and knowing and demonstrates social negotiations that are indicative of a better understanding of being part of a social group. For the school-age child, a successful classroom experience is predicated on being comfortable with and accepted by peers. Because peers are so important to the well-being of school-age children, poor social skills will be a major interference in cognitive growth and development. Poplin and Weeres (1993) state that "What matters most in schooling are essential human issues—concerns related, for example to human relationships, racial and cultural differences, values, safety and the aesthetic environment of the classroom."

Homogeneous groupings within the integrated classroom are used specifically for the direct teaching of needed skills, whether they be cognitive or social. For example, a small group of children are found to have difficulties in forming good questions about the material they are reading. By working with this group around this particular issue, the teacher can focus on a specific difficulty without having the distraction of children who are already accomplished at this task. Another example of a homogeneous grouping is to group children who are generally at the same developmental level together for purposes of extending their understanding of content as well as their role within the group.

Children should have, in any given day, time when they work with a few other children, a large group, and work alone. It is not desirable to always put children into a position in which interaction with others is necessary for the completion of a task or project, as it limits children's opportunities for self-reflection and the development of a metacognitive understanding of their abilities in a particular area. Large groups provide opportunities for learning to share, learning to listen, learning to respect others' points of view, and for gathering information and ideas which stimulate further thinking. Small groups require more interaction than the large group, putting more of a demand on the individual child for participation. Large groups permit a child to "rest" and be a more passive recipient. Each kind of grouping has particular strong points to offer a child and therefore must be considered by the teacher as he or she plans the day.

Explaining the Integrated Classroom to Others

If the teacher is clear on the philosophy and theory behind the integrated approach, it becomes easier for him or her to articulate the goals, and to tie these goals to those considered important to a particular school community. Basic to the integrated approach are two concepts previously discussed: "less is more" and the "subordination of teaching to learning." The teacher might explain the concept of less is more by demonstrating how a theme study involves and engages children in an in-depth understanding of the topic, and explaining how a theme study is less concerned with "covering" a given amount of material, which may be superficially understood. Some important aspects of "less is more" are the development of critical thinking, the ability to make connections between disciplines, the relevance to real life, the ability to become a good researcher, and the many opportunities for children to demonstrate their knowledge in a variety of ways, which come from taking more time with fewer but more meaningful topics during the school year.

The "subordination of teaching to learning" puts the focus on the child. The teacher might explain this by discussing how individual children have different ways of understanding and knowing, and how different children need different periods of time for the learning process. The teacher might discuss the concept of multiple intelligences and developmental appropriateness. The teacher can explain that he or she is not driven by time or content, but rather by what individual children need and the best ways to address these needs to ensure learning for understanding.

The integrated classroom, as described in this book, is a total approach to the development of the learning environment. For the teacher who is explaining this approach to others, it is important that he or she make clear how the physical environment, curriculum, family grouping, time frames, and instructional strategies interrelate to each other and to the cognitive and social/emotional development of the child. The teacher might explain how provisioning the environment supports independent learning, and how multi-age classrooms reflect the social groupings of the real world where individuals play, learn, and work together to accomplish a goal. He or she may also point out that the curriculum supports and encourages critical thinking, reflection, discovery, inquiry, the development of communication skills, and other necessary social competencies for appropriate group interactions.

The teacher should emphasize that the integrated approach is not limited to learning within the four walls of the classroom, but instead encourages community participation in many ways. The children use the community as part of their resource for research, observation, and materials. Resourceful community members are brought into the classroom to extend the children's understanding of how what they are learning fits into the real world. A community member might actually spend an extended period of time in the classroom, offering expertise and becoming part of the teaching/learning team.

For those that ask the teacher, "What about the basics?" the teacher might reply that children learn best through active involvement, in high-interest activities, in which they are challenged sufficiently but at the same time in ways that match their developmental levels. Through these activities, children learn basic skills in all academic areas, and these skills can be observed by examining their writing samples, their research projects, and their processfolios and portfolios. The teacher might add that the integrated approach does not preclude specific skill teaching when necessary, such as teaching the concept of percents when a child wants to create a circle graph relating to a particular theme study. The key is that children are motivated to learn because what they are learning is meaningful and relevant to their goals. In the integrated classroom, the teacher's goals and the children's goals are made compatible, so there is no need for an external reward system to get children to comply, and discipline problems are minimized.

The teacher can stress that in the integrated classroom there is more time for actual learning because children are more likely to stay focused, and that more experienced children are there to assist and lead those less experienced. Children become more responsible learners because of their participation in the planning process, and because the teacher acts as coach and guide, rather than director. Through this process, children learn to trust themselves, to take risks, and to recognize that making a mistake is part of learning.

Lastly, the teacher may want to emphasize that education for today's children, who will be the adults of the twenty-first century, must prepare them for a complex society which will require advanced problem-solving skills and the ability to be a productive member of a team. The complexity of the society of the twenty-first century will require individuals to have strengths in a variety of intelligences, and schools of today must find ways of supporting and strengthening all of these intelligences.

Gathering and Sharing Resources

The integrated classroom requires a variety of materials and resources, but these materials and resources do not have to be expensive. Many materials can be found by searching out discards from local businesses, asking parents for household throwaways, and trading with other teachers. The teacher should keep a resource file which provides information as to where to locate particular items, and as these resources are acquired, the file can be updated. Once a resource file is constructed, it becomes easier to acquire the necessary materials.

Basic supplies may be available from local businesses, professionals, medical offices, hospitals, print shops, frame shops, computer users, restaurants, tailors or dressmakers, florists, packing houses, travel agencies, pet shops, and lumber yards. These supplies may be donated or provided at minimal cost. Given the limited time teachers have, acquisition of materials can become a class project, with children identifying their needs, researching sources, and writing letters of request. In addition, the teacher, in his or her interactions with the community, can make his or her classroom's needs known. Often excellent sources of materials are unaware that what was to be discarded can become an integral part of an activities-based classroom. Some suggestions are:

computer runoffs	old stethoscopes and microscopes
cardboard boxes	
cardboard inserts	buttons
matte board	milk crates
newspapers and newsprint	tiles
paper of varied sizes, weights, and colors	carpet samples
	wallpaper samples
old restaurant menus	wood scraps
tongue depressors	calendars, old and current
travel posters and brochures	magazines, present and past issues
remnants of material	blueprints

Parents are an excellent resource for all kinds of materials—"throwaways," recyclables, and recently replaced items. Some of these materials include:

plastic containers of all sizes and shapes	cookie cutters
	ingredients for cooking
measuring cups and spoons	recipes
empty milk cartons of all sizes	old small appliances that may or may not work
discarded clothing	
old material	greeting cards
yarn	packaging materials
threads	wrapping paper
toilet paper and paper towel rolls	old tools
magazines	boxes of various shapes and sizes
cooking utensils	books

Sharing resources with colleagues can be both helpful and time-saving. While many materials (see "raw materials" in Chapter 3) are consumable and need constant replacement, others can be shared between two or more classrooms with relative ease. It is helpful if the classrooms that plan to be part of the sharing network develop both a resource list of the materials themselves and a schedule of when they can be available.

Reference Materials for the Integrated Classroom: Curriculum, Environmental Design, and the Role of the Classroom Teacher

Classroom Environment

Loughlin, Catherine E. and Suina, Joseph H. (1982). *The Learning Environment: An Instructional Strategy.* New York: Teachers College Press.

This book defines the learning environment and gives detailed guidelines on how the physical environment can support the teacher and children as they interact with each other and the materials. It specifically offers suggestions for organizing space and arranging materials, as well as defining the kinds and variety of provisions, including raw materials, tools, information sources, storage containers, individual and group work spaces, and displays. At the end of each chapter, there are suggestions for evaluating your own classroom and for making the desired changes. The text is liberally illustrated with simple drawings that support a well-organized classroom where children are independent learners.

Loughlin, Catherine E. and Martin, Mavis D. (1987). *Supporting Literacy: Developing Effective Learning Environments.* New York: Teachers College Press.

The focus of *Supporting Literacy* is the use of the physical environment to influence behavior and the acquisition of literacy. The book provides detailed information as to how to arrange a "functional literacy environment," which requires using environmental influences to promote established goals. It suggests an environment that matches individual differences and abilities while supporting self-initiated activity, and takes the position that children construct their own language growth. Although this book looks specifically at one aspect of curriculum, there are many ideas, examples, and assessment tools for a teacher who wishes to maximize the influence of the environment.

Theme Studies

Fredericks, Anthony D., Meinbach, Anita Meyer, and Rothlein, Liz. (1993). *Thematic Units.* New York: Harper Collins College Publishers.

The first part of this book discusses the concept of the thematic approach and gives a good overview of how the thematic approach relates to specific content areas. It then goes on to describe in-depth thematic units in science and social studies, utilizing whole language as the underlying structure. Journal writing is basic to all the activities described as are a wide selection of related works of literature. There are specific "culminating activities" suggested, as well as ideas for evaluation. Also included are many suggestions and forms for keeping track of children's work and for teacher evaluation of specific themes undertaken.

Gamberg, Ruth, Kwak, Winniefred, Hutchings, Meredith, and Altheim, Judy. (1988). *Learning and Loving It.* New Hampshire: Heinemann Educational Books, Inc.

The theme study approach is described from its inception to its completion. There are many examples of how to approach a theme study, as well as actual themes for different age groups. A strong point of this book is the section that deals with teachers' and parents' concerns regarding the acquisition of basic skills, evaluation, discipline, and the teacher's role in the theme study approach. Examples of children's work adds richness and offers opportunities for the reader to understand the value of the theme approach from a child's perspective. This is an outstanding and comprehensive resource which should be in the library of every teacher wanting to do theme studies.

Jacobs, Heidi Hayes, Ed. (1989). *Interdisciplinary Curriculum: Design and Implementation.* Virginia: Association for Supervision and Curriculum Development.

This is a collection of articles that help to demystify the design and implementation of an integrated curriculum. It offers a good background in the theory and rationale behind this approach. It presents a step-by-step approach to integration, and offers numerous suggestions for making curriculum integration successful. Jacobs defines the integrated model in several different ways, and gives both the positive and negative aspects of each.

Thompson, Gare. (1991). *Teaching Through Themes.* New York: Scholastic Professional Books.

An interesting section of this book describes learning strategies that can be observed through a theme study approach. There is also a short section about where to find themes which can be helpful for a teacher just beginning this process. Themes are categorized according to ideas such as people, friendship, and habitats for younger children. Theme ideas for older children become more abstract and include titles such as courage and survival.

Integrated Curriculum Units

AIMS (Activities in Mathematics and Science) (1988). California, Aims Education Foundation: Fresno, California.

AIMS features units which integrate mathematics, science, language arts, and social studies investigations for levels from kindergarten through grade 9. There is a series for primary grades, one for upper elementary, and one for middle level. Each unit covers topics of real-world concern to children, and uses materials which are easily obtained by the classroom teacher. These units are high interest and help to develop positive attitudes towards the study of mathematics and science for all children.

Elementary Science Study (ESS) Science Units. Delta Education, Inc., Dept. CB031, Box 950, Hudson, New Hampshire 03051.

These units, while basically science-oriented, incorporate a much broader view, and emphasize higher-order thinking skills, inquiry, and hypothesis-building. These units also encourage thoughtful, reflective writing and a variety of ways of representing work and conclusions.

GEMS (Great Explorations in Math and Science). California, Lawrence Hall of Science, University of California, Berkeley. Order information (415) 642–7771.

This is a series of integrated mathematics and science units for grades preschool–10. Some of the titles include Acid Rain, Experimenting with Model Rockets, Hide a Butterfly, Mapping Animal Movements, and Involving Dissolving. In addition to the guides, there are supplementary materials available for teachers and parents. These units are designed to meet the standards put forth in a report entitled Project 2061 published by the American Association for the Advancement of Science. A major focus is the development of an attitude of inquiry and excitement towards the sciences in children.

The Key School, Indianapolis, Indiana, the first elementary school predicated on Gardner's multiple intelligence theory, offers a publication entitled, *Connections, Patterns, Changes in Time and Space,* which features the three themes they use during the school year. For example, for the academic year 1987 to 1988, the three themes included "Connections," "Animal Patterns," and "Changes in Time and Space." Themes address specific intelligences which are noted at the end of each activity related to the theme. This school now has several more publications documenting their themes over the past several years.

The Voyage of the Mimi is a publication of the Bank Street College Project in Science and Mathematics. It is distributed through Wings for Learning,

Incorporated, 1600 Green Hills Road, Post Office Box 660002, Scotts Valley, California 95067 (800) 321–7511.

This fascinating integrated study incorporates a fictional story about counting and identifying the whale population off the coast of New England with videotaped factual documentation of particular scientific researchers in the story. There are discussion guides, hands-on activities, and computer software to augment the basic study. While the study is aimed at the upper elementary/middle school population, with modification it has been used successfully by teachers of younger children.

The Second Voyage of the Mimi focuses on Central America, and is an archeological study of existing ruins. The two main characters remain the same, making a connection with the first study. Each study also includes a crew member who has some form of physical disability: in Voyage I, one crew member is hearing impaired. In Voyage II, another crew member has lost a leg.

Integrating Activities

Dunn, Susan and Larson, Rob. (1990). *Design Technology: Children's Engineering*. Pennsylvania: The Falmer Press.

This book is about children's creative approach to planning and constructing a wide variety of objects, using junk materials. The authors show how to guide children through the planning process, make beginning sketches, organize their construction needs, do the actual building, and then review the product. The book has excellent visuals that clearly show children's work from beginning to end. In addition, the book provides excellent examples of brainstorming both in written and pictorial form. Brainstorming is an excellent method for helping children see relationships between and within content areas. This book does an excellent job of showing how to use children's interest in building and constructing in a way that is fun and meets academic standards.

Figure 7-1 (see page 170) is an example from this book of a brainstorm on "systems" that uses both words and pictures (p. 38).

This book provides several simple ways that children can be involved in the papermaking process. It provides a clear explanation of what paper is, and how papermaking developed over time. Natural extensions from this book could include a history of paper, a study of fibers, ecological considerations and concerns, research into how different kinds of paper has met different needs over time, and the uses to which paper is put today.

Johnson, Paul. (1992). *Pop-up Paper Engineering: Cross-Curricular Activities in Design Technology, English and Art*. Pennsylvania: The Falmer Press.

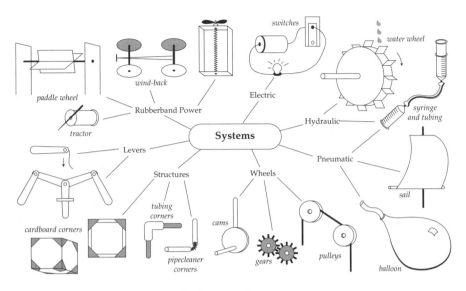

FIGURE 7-1   Brainstorm of "Systems"

Source: Dunn, Susan and Larson, Rob (1990), *Design Technology: Children's Engineering.*
Pennsylvania: The Falmer Press, p. 38.

This book is particularly good for building children's visual-spatial intelligence. There are a variety of activities which require children to apply conceptualization, manipulation, imaging, and visualization skills while constructing three-dimensional projects. Often opportunity for increasing the visual-spatial intelligence is limited. This intelligence is necessary for successful negotiation of the physical world and an appreciation of form. *Pop-up Paper Engineering* provides a good source of appropriate activities that will enhance a child's ability to think about objects in space and how they can be visually portrayed. Because of the emphasis on visual representation, there are many ways that children can use their creativity to express their ideas. Suggestions are made for evaluation and for cooperative learning.

Kalter, Joan Marie. (1989). *The World's Best String Games.* New York: Sterling Publishing Co.

Children the world over play string games. Using string games in the classroom opens the door for studying children from other cultures, and linking children with one another. String games provide many opportunities for storytelling and cooperative experiences. These games are also excellent for improving children's bodily kinesthetic intelligence by increasing their hand-eye coordination, and also enhances the visual-spatial intelligence by requiring that children be able to envision what will happen when the fingers are placed in specific situations to create new patterns. There are many diagrams in this book to assist both the teacher and child in playing the games.

Other Good Sources

Educational Leadership, published by the Association for Supervision and Curriculum Development (ASCD), is another source of outstanding articles on school restructuring, teacher professional development, assessment, and curriculum. For information, write to ASCD, 1250 North Pitt Street, Alexandria, Virginia 22314–1453.

Kappan is the title of a journal that is published monthly by Phi Delta Kappa. It frequently carries articles about authentic assessment, new models of education, and curriculum. Phi Delta Kappa, Inc., 408 North Union, P.O. Box 789, Bloomington, Indiana 47402.

Brendtro, Larry K., Brokenleg, Martin and Van Bockern, Steve. (1990). *Reclaiming Youth at Risk.* Indiana: National Educational Service.

This is an excellent source for understanding the ecological hazards that put children and youth "at risk." It provides a concept of risk that avoids blaming the child. This book supports teachers in providing what the authors call a "reclaiming environment"; one that creates changes which meet the needs of children in today's society.

Collis, Mark and Dalton, Joan. (1990). *Becoming Responsible Learners: Strategies for Positive Classroom Management.* New Hampshire: Heinemann Educational Books, Inc.

This is a simple but well-written book that provides practical information on how to encourage independent learners who take responsibility for their own behavior and are sensitive to the needs of others. This book takes a very humanistic approach to the area of classroom management and discipline, particularly with younger children.

Duckworth, Eleanor. (1987). *"The Having of Wonderful Ideas" and Other Essays on Teaching and Learning.* New York: Teachers College Press.

Duckworth presents an excellent understanding of Piaget's theory and its application to the classroom. She offers specific examples of how to successfully use cognitive conflict to help children move to the next level of thinking. Her book emphasizes that children, when presented with an environment appropriate to their developmental level, including a sensitive teacher, will successfully direct and construct their own learning experiences.

Ellis, Susan S. and Whelan, Susan F. (1990). *Cooperative Learning: Getting Started*. New York: Scholastic Press.

A good book for those who are just beginning to use cooperative learning strategies. It is written simply and straightforwardly, giving many specific examples of how to implement a cooperative structure.

Gardner, Howard. (1991). *The Unschooled Mind: How Children Think and How Schools Should Teach*. New York: Basic Books.

This is another excellent book which stresses the importance of understanding how children think and how, with an environment that is supportive of their thinking processes, they can successfully direct their own learning with a minimum of interference. This book validates for teachers the idea that children can be trusted to be self-motivated and to search out experiences that meet their learning needs. Gardner posits that as children explore the world, they develop robust (although primitive) theories of how the world works, which serve them well for many years. And if these "primitive" theories are not built upon in a more structured, scientific manner that leads to real understanding, they can and do continue to surface. Gardner also presents a new picture of child development, one in which children appear to show "waves" of development rather than invariant "stages" as Piaget stated.

Gardner, Howard. (1993). *Multiple Intelligences: The Theory in Practice*. New York: Basic Books.

This book carefully describes the theory of multiple intelligences and gives specific examples of how the research on these intelligences is being conducted. It further describes "the school of the future" in terms of the types of learning experiences children should have in order for them to acquire real understanding of subject matter. Gardner also lists many sources of information on the multiple intelligences, ranging from schools currently using this theory to individual researchers whose interest may lie with a particular age group or intelligence.

For those who might want to read more about how Gardner developed and researched his theory on multiple intelligences, we highly recommend *Frames of Mind*, published in 1983, also by Basic Books.

Jervis, Kathe and Montag, Carol. (Eds.) (1991). *Progressive Education for the 1990s: Transforming Practice*. New York: Teachers College Press.

This book is a collection of writings by authors whose interest in progressive education is reflected in their perspective that we need to rethink the tenets of this movement as it relates to issues of today. It is divided into three sections: a historical perspective, foundations for understanding, and the progressive high school. While this book does not place any particular emphasis on elementary education, it does provide the reader with an updated view of an educational concept which fostered the British Integrated Day.

Johnson, David W. and Johnson, Roger T. (1991). *Learning Together and Alone*. Massachusetts: Allyn and Bacon.

These authors are well known for their excellent and extensive work in the area of cooperative learning. This particular book seems to synthesize much of their previous work into one comprehensive volume dealing with all aspects of competitive, individual, and cooperative learning. As they state, they are not against competition, only inappropriate competition; and the research suggests that most competition in the classroom is inappropriate. They provide detailed suggestions for structuring each kind of learning in the classroom so that positive outcomes result, as well as a final section on "teacher concerns" about cooperative learning. This is a really good resource, not only for practical ideas using these three instructional strategies, but also as background support that can be used when explaining cooperative learning to parents and administration

Osterman, Karen F. (1990). Reflective Practice: A New Agenda for Education. *Education and Urban Society,* 22, 133–152.

This is a fairly detailed article that discusses in depth reflective practice and speaks to the importance of teachers being cognizant of their decisions, reactions, and responses, utilizing this information as important to an ongoing assessment and revision of existing theories of action. The emphasis of this article is on the importance of reflection as a major component of professional growth.

Perrone, Vito. (Ed.) (1991). *Expanding Student Assessment*. Virginia: ASCD.

This publication is a collection of writings from some of the foremost thinkers in the area of assessment today. The topics range from "Authentic Assessment: Beyond the Buzzword" to such areas as "The Intellectual Costs of Secrecy in Mathematics Assessment," and "Active Assessment for Active Science." The final chapter deals with "Moving Toward More Powerful Assessment," which pulls together the ideas presented in the previous chapters. The booklet is especially helpful for teachers who want specific direction in moving away from traditional practices.

Reid, Joanne, Forrestal, Peter and Cook, Jonathan. (1989). *Small Group Learning in the Classroom*. New Hampshire: Heinemann Educational Books, Inc.

This short, easy-to-read book is particularly helpful in providing many illustrations of appropriate ways to set up a physical environment that will support cooperative learning. In addition, the book gives a nice overview of issues to consider related to this particular instructional strategy.

Western Regional Center For Drug Free Schools and Communities. (August 1991). *Fostering Resiliency in Kids: Protective Factors in the Family, School, and Community.* Oregon: Northwest Regional Education Laboratory.

This publication provides an excellent review of research related to resiliency in children. It clearly describes those factors in the environment that support resiliency in the face of situations that put children at risk. It offers the teacher concrete ways of incorporating these supportive, protective factors in the classroom.

Examples of Brainstorms and Theme Studies

Shown in Figure 7-2(a–c) are examples of brainstorms that were developed with children by apprentice teachers from the College of Santa Fe Elementary Education Program. Brainstorms are one way of beginning theme studies that help children and teachers to organize the ways in which they will pursue both the topic and its subtopics. Brainstorms provide a visual way of seeing the connection between content areas or between concepts within the topic. These particular brainstorms were created with children in multi-age K-1-2 classrooms. They include not only the main topic brainstorm (Children Around the World) but also the subtopic brainstorms, which seem to illustrate best how brainstorming evolves. After brainstorming, groups of children decide which specific aspect of the theme they wish to research. Activities, materials, and resources are then made available for these groups to use. Once the research is accomplished, children demonstrate and share what they have learned so that all members of the class have access to the information.

An example of a theme study that takes a true interdisciplinary approach is "The Race Around the World." This theme study, for upper elementary children, asks that children become reporters for a world news magazine, and encourages their travel "around the world," researching any aspect of the countries in which they find themselves located. This theme study was originally designed to be a competitive effort, with each child seeing how many countries they could travel through and research, with the objective being to get all around the world. However, apprentice teachers and children have restructured it to be an excellent cooperative group study.

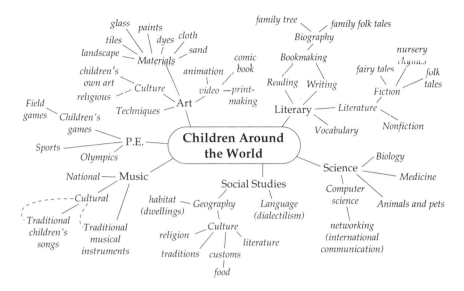

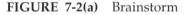

FIGURE 7-2(a)　Brainstorm

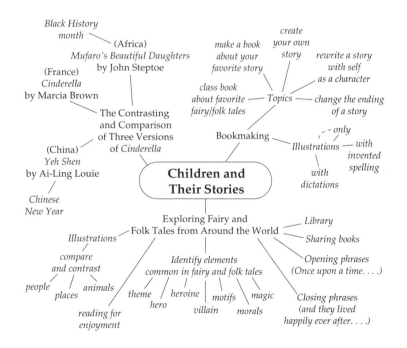

FIGURE 7-2(b)　Subtopic Brainstorms

FIGURE 7-2(c)   Brainstorming with the Class

The children "become" correspondents for a national news magazine entitled *Global Issues*. Each child, or team of children, is dropped into the capital city of a foreign country, with an initial check for expense money to get started. The correspondents then begin to research the country, writing articles, reviews, descriptions, or making maps, charts, graphs, or other visual representations for possible publication in *Global Issues*. The teacher acts as "editor," helping each child to create an interesting, noteworthy piece of work, for which the child is "paid" by check. Each time a correspondent moves to a new location, a trip planning sheet must be filed with the editor. The correspondent must also keep a personal ledger of all monies earned and all travel expenses paid out as he or she travels around the world. A travel chart listing ways of travel available in each country and the cost of each gives the children the information they need to choose their mode of travel. Their choices depend both on how much money they have earned and what country they are visiting. For example, travel by camel or yak can occur only within countries that use that method of transportation. Each type of travel offered has a specific cost per mile, and the correspondent must figure out his or her travel costs. Included at the end of this chapter are the trip planning sheet, the travel costs chart, the team summary sheet, the personal ledger, and checks for expenses (see pages 179–182). Below is a list of questions that can be suggested as research topics within various countries. It has been our experience that children use the list only as the study begins: as they get further and further into it, they begin to generate topics and questions on their own. This study was designed to be done over one semester. Again, we have found that most children want to continue it—sometimes over an entire year!

Question Suggestions

1. Is there a major mountain range that passes through your country? What other countries does it pass through? What are some of its most famous peaks? How has this range affected the history, economy, relations with other countries, etc.? How do you think this country might be different if the mountains were not there?
2. How does the climate affect the selection of crops grown in your country?
3. What are some of your country's minerals? What are they used for? Can you find out which countries buy them?
4. Draw or trace a map of your country. Be sure to include the scale of miles. What is the north–south maximum distance? East–west? Why do you think the capital is located where it is?
5. What holidays are celebrated in your country? How? Why?
6. Make a currency-conversion table for your country.
7. What are some of the unusual foods eaten in your country? Find a recipe for one of them. Make it and bring it in so we can taste it! (Not required)
8. Make a scale drawing of an important building in your country.
9. Write a personal adventure that happened to you in this country. Be sure to include lots of details about life in this country.
10. Retell some folktales and legends of the people in your country.
11. Describe an unusual sport or game played in this country. Be sure to include the rules. Teach some others in the class how to play the game. (Not required)
12. Submit a question you think would be a good one to research. Outline how you would go about producing this article.

If none of these appeal to you, think up some questions you would like to follow up on during the time we are doing this theme study.

Several teachers have added interesting components to the story to enhance its realism: issuing a simulated passport, which gets an interesting stamp added for each country visited (children design the stamps); publishing *Global Issues* monthly (quite easy today with all of the desktop publishing programs available to schools); and having older children keep records of all expenses (food, lodging, and meals as well as travel) over the course of the study. Teachers make their own decisions on how much is to be paid for each piece of work; we only wish to underscore the need to give as much attention (and reward) to maps, graphs, drawings, and charts as for written articles, so that children's visual-spatial intelligence can be honored on an equal footing with their linguistic intelligence. It is important to keep in mind that the ability to create a good map, an informative graph or chart, or a drawing is as difficult as writing. If *Global Issues* is published monthly or even bimonthly, new "jobs" can be created for which children should be paid: local news editor, national news editor, world news editor, layout specialists, type setters (computer typists), and so on.

We unfortunately don't know the origin of this wonderful idea. It has traveled around this country to and through a great many schools, each adding and changing the format slightly to fit its particular population. The idea is not ours; we encountered it back in the seventies when there was a surge of interest in Integrated classrooms in this country. So—cheers to whomever is its originator! It is an excellent theme study, and has never failed to excite and interest children wherever it has been used.

These resources, references, and examples are our favorites. There are many, many more publications and sources of information that are interesting, helpful, and supportive of making substantive changes in today's classrooms.

References

Gamberg, Ruth, Kwak, Winniefred, Hutchings, Meredith, and Altheim, Judy. (1988). *Learning and Loving It.* New Hampshire: Heinemann Educational Books.

Jacobs, Heidi Hayes. ed. (1989). *Interdisciplinary Curriculum: Design and Implementation.* Virginia: Association for Supervision and Curriculum Development.

Poplin, Mary and Weeres, Joseph. (1993). Listening at the Learner's Level. *The Executive Educator.* April, p. 14–19.

GLOBAL ISSUES NEWS SERVICE
Trip Planning Sheet

Correspondent _____ _____   Date _____

Totals to date:

Current bank balance $ _____

Miles traveled _____   Days traveled _____

Number of countries visited _____

Number of cultural areas visited _____

Travel plans:

I am presently in _____ , _____ .
City   Country

I plan to travel to _____ , _____ .
City   Country

The distance on the map is _____ inches.

The real distance is _____ miles.

_____ miles are over water and _____ miles are over land.

I plan to travel by:

Method	Number of miles	Number of days	Cost per mile	Total

The total cost of the trip will be $ _____ . It will take _____ days.

After the trip my totals to date should read:

Total miles traveled _____

Total traveling days _____

Total countries visited _____

Total cultural areas visited _____

My new bank balance is $ _____ .

TRAVEL COSTS CHART

Method	Cost/Mile	Miles/Day
Airplane	0.25/mile	1500
Train	0.11/mile	800
Steamship	0.09/mile	800
Sailboat	0.07/mile	350
Taxi	0.84/mile	575
Elephant	0.06/mile	47
Yak	0.05/mile	66
Llama	0.08/mile	68
Horse	0.13/mile	52
Camel	0.04/mile	49
Rickshaw	0.01/mile + 15% tip	22

TEAM SUMMARY SHEET NO. _____

Team Members:

_____

_____

_____

_____

_____

Total countries visited:

Total miles traveled _____

Total number of days spent traveling _____

Kinds of transportation used _____

_____

_____

Total number of articles, charts, graphs, etc. accepted

_____

Total amount earned for reporting $ _____

PERSONAL LEDGER

Name _____

Date	Credit/article or graphic	Debit/travel costs	$ Credit	$ Debit
	Totals			

GLOBAL ISSUS INC.   *check number* _____
1000 Washington Way
New York, N.Y. 12345-6789   _____ 19 _____
(333) 211-3115

Pay to the order of _____ $ _____

_____ *Dollars*

Nofunds National Bank
1111 Anstreet
Anywhere, N.Y. 87505-1122

Memo _____   _____
                                          Editor

8

Questions and Answers:
A Summary

Excellence can be achieved if you care more than others think is wise, and you risk more than others think is safe! (Anonymous)

It is expected that when a teacher chooses to implement a theory fundamentally different from currently accepted practice, questions will be raised by other teachers, administrators, parents, and children. Although not every possible question is addressed in this chapter, the most commonly asked questions are included with responses to assist the teacher in clarifying, for him- or herself and others, the philosophy, rationale, and value of the integrated approach.

Questions from Teachers

1. If I choose to implement this approach in my classroom, what do I do about an administration, parents, and other colleagues who are resistant to this change?

First, it is critical that the teacher understand clearly what he or she expects this approach to accomplish that his or her current methodology does not. Outcomes must be linked to outcomes expected by the administration and parents. It is just as critical that the teacher have an understanding and an appreciation of how children learn within a developmental framework, so that he or she can advocate for appropriate classroom practices. Often a teacher using an innovative approach finds that part of his or her responsibility is to teach others about the value of this approach. To do this, the teacher must be able to: (1) direct interested parents and colleagues to the research that supports the approach, (2) provide examples of children's learning, and (3) demonstrate through the design and provisioning of the room, curriculum content, and his or her own interactions with children, how the model unfolds. The teacher may also want to make small but persistent changes, demonstrating in an ongoing way the success of the approach. Having children's finished projects, investigations, journals, and portfolios available can provide a great deal of information about and support for children's learning. Resistance to change is often a result of feeling as though the change is being imposed without regard to concerns, beliefs, and practices of others. Including administration, colleagues, and parents in the process of change helps to ensure that everyone has a stake in the outcomes.

Because it is sometimes difficult for others to accept and support changes that are outside the realm of their own personal experience, the teacher may have to accept that some colleagues and parents may adopt a wait-and-see attitude, and may not be as supportive as the teacher would like. It can be helpful if the teacher is able to find an ally within the school to act as a support, and also to help the teacher find ways of explaining and demonstrating the positive effects of the change in a manner that is non-threatening. Ideally, if two or three teachers begin this process together, they can be mutually supportive and offer even more objective data to assist others in evaluating the pros and cons of an integrated classroom.

2. What do I do with reluctant children?

The integrated classroom requires that children be responsible, independent learners. For some children, this is a new experience. These children may not be adept at making choices, directing their own learning, or negotiating the social aspects of the classroom. The teacher must take the time to teach children *how* to function successfully in this environment. This may mean initially giving specific children more direction, gradually increasing their responsibility and choices, and offering opportunity to learn and practice appropriate social skills.

It may take some children time to trust themselves as learners. In the more traditional classroom, children are not asked to take as many risks as "owners" of their learning process. The teacher can be helpful to these children by providing specific feedback to them about their learning process and about the expected outcomes. In addition, the teacher can support risk-taking by providing many opportunities for success in this new environment. Upper elementary children may be negatively influenced by others to think of their classroom as a place for playing rather than learning, because they are not obligated to follow a predetermined time frame or participate in the more traditional teacher-directed lessons. The teacher should explain to children, as he or she does to parents and colleagues, the expected outcomes of this approach and how the activities address those outcomes.

Further, children need to adjust their attitudes towards and expectations of the purpose of school. Most children, by grade 3 or 4, have a fixed idea of school being a place where they are passive recipients of teacher knowledge, and where space is defined individually by desks and chairs. Children are often reluctant to consider the classroom as shared space: the idea of a community of learners needs to be established.

3. We are a poor school district with few supplies, and our Board of Education requires that we use the standard textbooks. How can I get the necessary materials and equipment, and what do I do about the textbooks?

There is no reason why textbooks cannot be incorporated as one of the resources used by teachers and children in the classroom. One way of doing this is to use the text as a reference for teacher planning to assure that the textbook material is addressed. Another approach is to have a particular time each day when text lessons are covered and, if required, workbook pages are completed. There is an excellent chapter detailing a sixth-grade teacher's shift from using traditional text material to an integrated, child-centered approach in Carl Rogers 1983 book, *Freedom To Learn*.

Refer to Chapter 7 for sources of possible free or inexpensive materials. Also, never hesitate to write to a company and ask for specific resources. An offer to provide feedback on children's use of these materials, can increase the likelihood of getting what is requested. Do not be deterred by a lack of materials or equipment. Needed materials can be borrowed, exchanged, or acquired at flea markets, garage sales, or through donations. Libraries often will allow teachers to select and keep for a month, books and other information sources that can be useful for investigations. The teacher can build an environment rich in materials over time. *Rarely* are classrooms provisioned the first year, or the first time, the way a teacher might want.

4. What do I do about basic furnishings?

One major change from a more traditional classroom setting is the idea that there are no individual desks. Flat-topped desks, however, can be used in a variety of groupings to create usable workspaces. The teacher's desk also can be used as a workspace by keeping it clear and putting it in a space that is accessible to children. Children's personal items are stored in cubbies or bins (see Chapter 3). Carpet samples can be used to define workspaces on the floor, as can pillows. Bricks and boards can be used for storage shelves and for provisioning different areas of the room, and also act as "dividers" for defining space. Large cardboard boxes can be used to provide spaces for children to be alone and also can be cut down to provide individual "carrels" on desk tops for reading or studying with minimal distraction. When teachers create very private spaces, the children within these spaces must always be within sight of the teacher. For example, height of the boxes, as well as their placement, must be carefully considered.

Trades with colleagues can provide tables of the right height, chairs, and bookcases for children of a variety of ages. It is important to have dividers which do not obstruct the teacher's ability to see and monitor all corners of the classroom.

If there are children in the classroom with specific physical disabilities, an excellent chapter in *The Learning Environment* (Loughlin and Suina, 1982) discusses modifying the environment to accommodate special needs.

   5. I'm not creative. How can I think of themes and curriculum content?

The teacher can begin by asking the children about their interests, and what they might like to learn. Using the children's own interests, the teacher can begin to consider how to accomplish the community's goals and objectives in meaningful ways. Referring back to Chapter 7, there are curricula available to help a teacher get started. Often, after beginning with one of these ready-made curricula, the teacher finds that he or she has generated many ideas of his or her own. These original ideas can extend and strengthen the published curricula

Brainstorming (again, refer to Chapter 7) is an excellent way to stimulate anyone's creativity. It encourages a free flow of ideas without evaluation. Brainstorms, as described in Chapter 2 of *Learning and Loving It*, are designed to assist in making connections between content and concepts, and provide a visual reminder of the ideas expressed. Posting brainstorms in an easily accessible place stimulates further thinking on the topic and provides more opportunities for the generation of ideas.

Teachers should keep an "idea" file to record thoughts, impressions, observations, those instantaneous decisions that yield really positive outcomes, resources, successful activities, and projects from colleagues. Teachers can then use these ideas as a beginning place for their creative problem solving in the development of themes and curricular activities.

   6. I am pressured to teach specific skills so that my children will do well on standardized tests. How do I make certain that these skills are learned?

One way is to make certain that when the teacher assesses children's learning, the particular skills of concern are demonstrated adequately by the children's projects, investigations, or both. This requires that teachers be able to clearly identify those skills that the child has mastered, as well as those needing more practice. In addition, documentation of skills learned, and those in process, is important so that the teacher can support the learning and application of these skills in a variety of ways. This documentation also is proof to parents and administrators that appropriate skills are being learned.

If children are required to take standardized tests, then the teacher has a responsibility to make certain that children know *how* to be successful test-takers. This requires that children learn how to follow directions and how to use the format employed by a particular test, such as true/false or multiple choice. Test-taking is a skill in itself, and requires instruction and practice.

As teachers become more comfortable in assessing and demonstrating children's learning in a variety of ways, they may wish to work with parents and their school district to reduce reliance on standardized tests. Standardized tests as the main way of evaluating children's learning have been proved to be limited as they do not address the process of learning and knowing. Gardner states:

In the course of their careers in the American schools of today, most students take hundreds, if not thousands, of tests. They develop skill to a highly calibrated degree in an exercise that will essentially become useless immediately after their last day in school. (Gardner, 1993, p. 114)

Teachers can assist parents and colleagues in understanding the developmental nature of skills acquisition, and that competencies must reflect not only this process, but that development often takes place over an extended span of time, not necessarily in accordance with specific grades or points during the year. It is helpful if teachers recognize that there is often a discrepancy between what a child can demonstrate and what a child truly understands. This reveals another problem inherent in standardized tests and assessments that address district-determined competencies or outcomes: children may be able to demonstrate the "correct" answer, but not have internalized the concept or the process.

7. Other teachers make me feel like I am wasting the children's time, and are annoyed with me, as they perceive that what I am doing requires a lot more time and effort and makes them look bad. How do I handle this?

The first thing a teacher must recognize is that having a firm belief in what he or she is doing is critical to withstanding pressure to conform. In addition, a teacher must be willing to take risks and to be responsible for carefully documenting the process and progress of change, so that he or she can be an educator to other educators. Having a knowledge base that is well-grounded in theory gives the teacher a more credible position. Modeling this approach successfully is crucial in assisting others in their understanding and acceptance. Inviting other teachers to observe, offering to assist others in getting started, possibly teaming with a teacher who is skeptical, can help reduce some of the negative feelings. A teacher may find that, no matter what he or she does to educate others about the model, some teachers will not agree that this approach is valid. A teacher may find him- or herself in the position of electing to use the integrated approach without the support or understanding of colleagues. For this teacher, there must be a strong conviction that this approach is the one that best addresses the children's needs. Again, documentation and reflection can help ensure that the teacher has objective information by which to assess his or her successes. In addition, this information can provide guidelines as to where the teacher needs to increase his or her own knowledge and skill. Teachers may also find colleagues who accept the approach as valid but are not comfortable with implementing the approach in their own classrooms. It is important to recognize that this approach requires that an individual teacher not only have a strong belief in the approach, but also a high degree of comfort in putting it into practice. Without the comfort level, it becomes easy to undermine the practice, and move towards failure rather than success.

This approach does take more time, especially in the beginning, but as a teacher becomes more comfortable and knowledgeable with the approach, it is less time-consuming. A teacher implementing this approach should recognize the initial time factor and be willing to give the time to establish the materials, resources, activities, and project possibilities. Once this is accomplished, the teacher's time and energy goes to the ongoing assessment and planning process which occurs as he or she interacts with and observes children throughout the day.

8. Parents want to know why children don't have homework in specific subjects.

Homework in specific subjects increases the probability that learning becomes fragmented and unrelated to real-world problem solving and application. Given the experiences children have during their school day, it is unnecessary for them to practice isolated skills. In the integrated classroom, there is actually more time spent on academic activities because time is not segmented: little time is wasted in transitions from one activity to another, children are actively engaged providing less opportunities for behavior problems, and teachers have more time to work directly with children and their immediate learning needs.

Appropriate homework for an integrated classroom might include research about a theme, interviews of community or family members, reading for pleasure as well as information, and collecting materials for projects or displays. Children and teachers may contract for specific after-school activities that will possibly involve older peers or parents, or be considered a service-oriented project. Sometimes a child's participation in an after-school activity such as a boy's or girl's club, scouts, or art or music classes can be incorporated as part of projects or themes in the classroom. Specific elements of these activities can become part of the homework assignment.

9. This is a competitive society. How will children using this cooperative approach be prepared to compete?

The first part of this question can be debated. There are many indications coming from the business world that, to remain competitive as a society in a global economy, we need individuals who understand how to work collectively as a team. Cooperative learning situations in the integrated classroom provide the skills and attitudes necessary to work effectively with others on projects in the workplace of the future. Aspects of the individual that will be important in the workplace of the future will be the expertise the individual brings to the team, and the ability of the individual to be a critical thinker and problem-solver. The integrated classroom prepares children to be cooperative collaborators, and at the same time, strengthens their individual intelligences, increases their understanding of their own competencies, and makes them more knowledgeable about what they have to offer the workplace of the future. Children in the integrated classroom work to improve and strengthen their own abilities independent of their peers, since the emphasis is on the individual's own developmental time table, and more often than not, children are working on different activities, at different levels, at the same time. These different activities at different levels may be part of a larger cooperative theme or project being undertaken by the class as a whole or a specific group. The focus of the integrated classroom is on the development of self, rather than on "besting" one's peers.

10. What do I do about children who complete their work quickly and easily? Will the the children who take more time hinder the progress of the faster students?

Because the integrated classroom does not require that every child end up with exactly the same amount of content knowledge, children who complete their work more quickly do not have to wait for other children to finish before going on to another activity or project. Children are encouraged to move at their own pace, and efforts on the part of one child to compete with another child are discouraged. Assignments are designed to meet the specific developmental needs of individual children, and therefore children are not often working on exactly the same problem. This does not mean that children are not working on the same concept at the same time, but rather that the approach or materials may differ. Even when there is an assignment that all children are exploring, the inquiry is open-ended enough so that children take their own pathways to its completion.

When more experienced children act as mentors or "teachers" for the less experienced, they must understand the material in a more sophisticated manner. This ensures that children who are assisting other children are still learning and developing further expertise. Having children with different levels of understanding in one classroom increases rather than decreases opportunities for the more advanced children to grow.

11. What do I do with a child whose interests seem very different from other children in the class?

In the integrated classroom, a child who has particular interests different from his or her peers is not looked upon as a problem. There is no effort made to force the child to conform to a particular curricular mold, or to study a predetermined content area in a predetermined way. This does not imply that children are not expected to learn a body of knowledge, specific concepts, or skills and attitudes. What it does imply is that the child's interests must be the guiding factor in determining how these components are acquired. For example, a particular child may not find any subtopic of a selected theme study of interest to her. She may then suggest alternative subtopics that are still related to the theme but will not be explored by any of the other children. The skills and concepts being used and explored are the same as those for other subtopics but the content of the child's choice draws her and keeps her engaged.

12. How do I encourage children to make choices without having chaos in my classroom?

The physical environment must be supportive of choice and the reduction of chaos. This means that workspaces are well-defined and appropriately provisioned (refer to Chapter 3). Materials should be seen easily and properly labeled so children can independently find, use, and replace them. Choices should be appropriate to developmental levels, and limited in number according to children's ability to use the materials. Too many choices can be overwhelming, causing children to act irresponsibly. Younger children need opportunities to learn how to make choices based on a plan of action and to follow through on evaluating the outcome of their choices. Teachers must be careful to offer only choices that they sincerely want the child to make. Sometimes choices are offered, but children are discouraged from selecting them. A good example of an inappropriate choice is a shelf full of games available to children; however when these games are chosen, the teacher suggests that the games are really for recess when the weather is poor. If something is in the classroom and in a place where it is available to children, it should be a valid choice. If there are materials or activities that the teacher wants reserved for special occasions, they should be kept in a place specifically reserved for the teacher.

Many children have had few opportunities for engaging in the process of choice. As with all new learning, developing the ability to make responsible choices requires instruction and practice. It is often necessary to begin with very limited choices, helping children to identify what they really want to pursue, the implications for the outcomes of choices, and the process by which the choice must be made. With upper elementary children who have come from a more traditional setting, having the opportunity to make many choices can be anxiety producing. Making a choice is taking a risk that the choice will not be acceptable or is really not considered "the best" choice out of those available. The teacher must make certain that all children are helped to identify their choices as valid, and that no choice is evaluated by the teacher as being being less valid than another. If the teacher makes a choice available, the teacher should have previously assessed the value of this choice and therefore should be comfortable with a child making this choice at any given time.

13. What will happen to my children if they move to a more traditional classroom?

The integrated classroom should prepare children to be flexible and sensitive to a multitude of environments. Children in these classrooms have opportunities to work alone, as well as with others. Although there is considerably less teacher-directed activity, there is some. Children do learn to follow directions, to wait their turn, to respect others' opinions, and to take part in large group interactions. Because these children develop into independent learners, they are more able to regulate their own behavior and their use of time, relying less heavily on teacher cues for what to do and when to do it. The traditional classroom may be frustrating for a child from an integrated classroom experience because of the difference in the level of physical activity, choice, and self-direction. If teachers in integrated environments know that some children in their classroom will be moving to traditional settings, they have a responsibility to prepare the children for the changes they will find. Teachers may find it necessary to actually "practice" with children some of the behaviors required in these classrooms. This may be particularly true for children in eight-, nine-, and ten-year-old multi-age classrooms who are moving on to middle schools.

14. Are there some teachers who do not do well in an integrated setting?

Yes! Just as there are teachers who do not do well in a traditional setting, some teachers do not do well in the integrated setting. To be successful in an integrated classroom, a teacher must be firmly grounded in a child-centered approach that is guided by developmental theory. He or she must take the position that children learn best by doing, and that children have within them the capacity and the desire to learn. The teacher must perceive children as being capable of self-direction without the necessity for external control and rewards. A teacher, to be successful with this approach, must be flexible and willing to change direction at a moment's notice according to the needs of children. The teacher must be comfortable sharing power with children. In addition, teachers using this approach must appreciate the concept of multiple intelligences and be willing to incorporate opportunities in the curriculum for all these intelligences to be developed. It is crucial that the teacher understand and be capable of using a variety of assessment tools, and be willing to engage in reflective practice since so much of what happens in the integrated classroom is subtle rather than overt, and subjective rather than objective.

Teachers who do best in this setting are more apt to find higher levels of activity and noise acceptable. They are comfortable with children moving about and doing many different things at any given time. They are also comfortable with the role as "coach" and observer, rather than dispenser of knowledge. Teachers in these classrooms tend to be interested in the process rather than just the product.

15. How does this approach fit with all the restructuring that is occurring in education today?

A major component of the restructuring movement is to move away from the factory model of education, in which skills are taught in isolation, in fragmented time frames, and in a context that is not relevant to the students' world. A prominent voice in the restructuring movement is Ted Sizer whose Re:Learning model has been adopted in many states and communities. Although Re:Learning is essentially a secondary movement, New Mexico has chosen to use this model in reforming elementary education. The "nine common principles" advocated by this movement clearly support the idea of integrated learning, the development of the child as problem-solver and researcher, the relevancy of education to the real world, and the teacher's role as facilitator of the child's learning process. The integrated classroom model requires that teachers have autonomy in selecting curriculum and methodology to meet stated community goals. This is congruent with another major aspect of restructuring movements, which are designed to give teachers and parents more say in how best to meet the needs of children in specific schools.

The integrated classroom requires that children be involved in active learning with high expectations, and that an enriched curriculum be implemented that focuses on higher-order thinking skills within a heterogeneous grouping. Levin's Accelerated Schools, which are involved in the restructuring movement, have similar requirements. The Accelerated Schools also incorporate peer tutoring and cooperative learning. Much of the restructuring movement is encouraging the use of alternative and authentic assessment, and diploma by exhibition rather than accumulated credit hours. In addition, major restructuring efforts, as do integrated classrooms, emphasize parent and community support, and the development of children who have a strong sense of themselves as competent learners, with a good understanding of their strengths, and the ability to act as a responsible member of a group.

16. What happens if I don't like a particular child and this child is assigned to me for three years? Or what if the child doesn't like me?

First, the teacher must recognize that liking every child is virtually impossible. There will always be some children that the teacher prefers over others. This is an important issue for teachers to consider, since they are often taught that they should "love" all children all of the time. When this does not happen a teacher may feel guilty or angry and not be able to achieve his or her goals with the particular child. For example, a guilty teacher may not hold a particular child to behavioral or academic expectations, frequently making excuses for the child, or giving the child more opportunities than others to conform. The angry teacher may distance him- or herself from the child, making it even more necessary for the child to engage in inappropriate interactions to gain the teacher's attention.

Sometimes it is helpful for teachers to keep a personal journal which describes, without evaluation, feelings and responses to children in their class, particularly for children difficult for them to like. Personal journals often provide teachers with insights that allow them to gain some objectivity about their feelings, and provide an opportunity to consider how they may respond in a more professional manner.

Another way of testing one's objectivity towards a child is to ask a colleague to come and observe for a period of time. This observation can provide important information about not only the child's behavior but also about the interactions of teacher and child. Sometimes the teacher can significantly change his or her behavior, so that the child's behavior changes in ways that makes the child more appealing to that teacher. When another person is not available, or if the teacher desires an extended observation, setting up a video camera can provide the needed feedback. If a video camera is not available, a tape recorder will provide information about "teacher talk," which includes tone of voice, use of language, hidden messages, kinds of questions, and length of time the teacher waits for a child to respond. A tape, either audio or video, also will give teachers feedback as to children's responses to the teacher as well as to other children. Both video and audio recordings can give insight into some of the subtle interactions between children. Sometimes a teacher will assume a particular child is causing a disruption, but in reality a quieter, less obvious child is at the root of the disturbance.

It is important for a teacher to know what behaviors of children are particularly salient to him or her, so that he or she can monitor his or her responses more sensitively. For some teachers, a child who is always asking questions, challenging directions, and following his or her own individual interests without discussing the possibilities with the teacher would be exciting and enjoyable. For other teachers, this particular child would be perceived as difficult and disruptive. A teacher may wish to look upon a "problem" with a particular child as an opportunity for self-reflection and growth, as well as an opportunity to model relationship building.

If a child and a teacher truly cannot find common ground for positive interactions, the teacher may be able to have the child moved to another classroom. This should not be viewed as a failure by either teacher or child, but rather as a necessary step for the comfort of both parties. In addition, when children are assigned to classrooms, the personalities of both children and teachers should be considered.

If a child does not like a teacher, it becomes the teacher's responsibility to try to understand the dynamics of the relationship and to adjust accordingly. Again, this can be a wonderful opportunity for both child and teacher to explore new ways of relating and behaving.

17. How does the integrated approach fit for a child who has behavioral or learning problems?

Often a child who has been identified as having a behavior or learning problem has been in classrooms which are unresponsive to his or her needs. Frequently these children are just "learning different," and their behavior problems are a result of inappropriate environments. This is just as true for children who sometimes seem "slow," unable to grasp concepts, exhibit poor memory, attention, or recall skills. Gardner also emphasizes the need for teachers to know several ways of teaching a concept or skill, so that children can use their strongest intelligences as the initial way to internalize the material. The integrated classroom, by its very nature, is designed to support different learning styles and time frames for internalization. The mixed-age group allows children to work with peers at comfort levels as well as with peers who will challenge and lead. Because the emphasis in this kind of classroom is children moving at their own pace, there is not the negative kind of comparison that one finds in a competitive classroom. This provides children with many opportunities to develop their personal sense of competence as learners and an understanding of how they learn most effectively. When children are given the chance to see themselves as succeeding rather than failing, their self-image improves, providing them with a sense of internal control. This perceived internal control becomes the basis of more self-directed and responsible behavior.

Children do come into classrooms with diagnosed learning disabilities and emotional problems. Many children today are classified as having Attention Deficit Disorder, with or without hyperactivity. Although not all of these children respond well to the integrated environment, this kind of classroom can be supportive and helpful to certain children when a more individualized approach is needed. For the child who shows hyperactivity, this classroom puts fewer demands on the child to sit still and attend without physical activity for long periods of time. This classroom also allows for more personal supervision and for the teacher to structure time, tasks, and workspace to assist the hyperactive child to be successful.

18. Are there children who might not do well in this type of classroom?

Yes! Some children may require more structure, more time-limited tasks, and more external controls. Some of these children might succeed in an integrated classroom if they are given enough opportunities to learn new ways of behaving and knowing. In addition, if parents, siblings, and peers in other types of classrooms do not truly understand the integrated approach, they can easily undermine a child's enthusiasm and success in this type of setting. For some parents, school means that children sit at desks, do predetermined tasks and pages in workbooks, and have homework assignments nightly that clearly demonstrate skills practice. Competition is an important element for some parents, as they see this as crucial for their child's success in the real world. Children may perceive school much as their parents do, and be unhappy in a setting different from what they expect. Children and parents must have some commitment to the integrated approach for it to work.

19. How do I explain the relationship between play and learning?

The word *play* has many connotations. Unfortunately, play has often been associated as a reward that follows work. Work is considered the really meaningful activity in this pair. In the traditional classroom, play is something that occurs at recess. In the integrated classroom, the word *play* has a broader connotation. Children play as scientists do, with ideas, materials, hypotheses, and outcomes, using play as a creative medium for investigations. Some of the dictionary synonyms for *play* include "enjoyment," "pleasure," "fun," "activity," and "to entertain oneself." A goal of the integrated classroom is to encourage lifelong learning. For this to happen, children need to perceive learning as an enjoyable, pleasurable activity. The reward that often follows "work" in the traditional classroom becomes the reward inherent in all activities of the integrated classroom. The idea that work has to be hard as well as unpleasant is debatable. Children in the integrated classroom work hard at their tasks, but because the tasks are interesting and presented in developmentally appropriate ways, they also are enjoyable. Children learn naturally through their interactions with materials, peers, and adults, that completing a project or task requires persistence, thought, responsibility, clear communication, and often doing things that are not always exciting but are necessary for successful completion.

It is important for the teacher to educate parents and colleagues to the nature of play in the integrated classroom. One way of doing this is to make a large chart to be posted just inside or outside the classroom door, entitled "Things to Watch for When Observing the Integrated Classroom." On it, list items such as the following:

1. Note how the teacher is not the center of attention, but is actively engaged.
2. See how children are working together or individually on a variety of tasks.
3. Note what specific skills children are using and what specific concepts children are learning.
4. Notice how children are actively involved in their activities.
5. Observe how children help each other.
6. Notice how children monitor their own behavior.

These are not the only things that can be listed on such a poster. Teachers may have specific things they want visitors to observe in their classrooms. What is critical for an outsider to consider is the overall involvement of the children in the various tasks, projects, and activities offered.

Another way of communicating the effectiveness of such a classroom is to have a "Parents Night," when parents are given the opportunity to participate actively, as their children would, in the classroom. After parents have experienced the classroom, the teacher can help the parents interpret the activities as to the concepts and skills that their children are learning. This may help parents understand more clearly the relationship between play and learning.

20. How do I explain to others that there are no failures in my classroom?

The integrated classroom strongly supports the premise that there are no failures, only different degrees of success. First, children who remain with the same teacher over the three-year age span become confident, competent learners. They trust not only the teacher but also the environment and themselves, and do not need to go through the yearly readjustment to a new room, new peers, a new teacher, new rules, and new expectations. This level of trust and comfort goes a long way toward supporting continued success with academic learning. Because children work on tasks and activities that are truly developmentally appropriate, there is less attrition in learning, which makes review and reteaching less necessary.

The integrated classroom provides more time for academic learning because it allows children extended time for work. There are few start/stop time periods, so the time taken in the traditional classroom for transitions, retrieval of texts, papers, and pencils, and direction-giving is minimized. Children have more opportunity to learn, practice, and extend their competencies.

The following quotation sums up the basic tenets of this book, and speaks to the essence of what should be the educational experience for the child:

> *The secret of Education lies in respecting the pupil. It is not for you to choose what he shall know, what he shall do. It is chosen and foreordained, and he holds the key to his own secret.*

> *Ralph Waldo Emerson*

Index